Your Journey to Visibility Workbook

A PROVEN ACTION PLAN TO ACHIEVE CAREER SUCCESS

SUSAN M. BARBER

Copyright © 2025 Susan M. Barber.

All rights reserved. No part or any portion of this book may be reproduced in any form, mechanical or digital, or transmitted without the prior written permission of the author, except for the use of brief quotations in a book review.

Some names and identifying details have been changed to protect the privacy of individuals.

This book is presented solely for educational and entertainment purposes. It is the author's intent to provide general knowledge and helpful information on the subjects discussed to assist readers in their quest for greater understanding and utilization of the ideas, thoughts, and principles presented. The advice and strategies contained herein may not be suitable for your situation.

ISBN: 978-1-7376104-0-3

Front cover image and book design by CB Messer

Edited by Zoë Bird

Proofread by KellyAnn Bessa

Printed in the United States of America.

First printing edition 2025

Susan M. Barber

Lake Villa, IL 60046

https://susanmbarber.com

*To the leaders who are ready to take a new journey
to show their value, build their confidence,
and make a visible impact now.*

Contents

INTRODUCTION 1

PART 1: VISIBILITY AND CAREER GROWTH FRAMEWORK 15
    Chapter 1: Step 1: Reflect—Where Did You Start? 17
    Chapter 2: Step 2: Review—Where Are You Now? 27
    Chapter 3: Step 3: Reimagine—Where Do You Want to Go? 43

PART 2: FOUNDATIONS FOR SUCCESS 61
    Chapter 4: Core Foundations 63
    Chapter 5: Personal Branding Foundation 97
    Chapter 6: Showing Value and Building
    Confidence Foundation 119

PART 3: ASSESS CHALLENGES AND TAKE ACTION 147
    Chapter 7: Step 4: Assess—What Path Is Best for You? 149
    Chapter 8: Step 5: Take Action—What Path Do You Choose? ... 155
    Chapter 9: The Communication / Clarity Solution Path 163
    Chapter 10: The Influencing / Relationships Solution Path 193
    Chapter 11: The Leading / Being Strategic Solution Path 211
    Chapter 12: The Journey Continues 231

APPENDIX 241

ACKNOWLEDGMENTS 245

ABOUT THE AUTHOR 247

ENDNOTES 249

Introduction

"Do you think I could be a leader? I never thought of myself as a leader," said a woman named Barbara who was sitting at the back of the room during a recent event. In response to my question to the attendees, "How do you want to be perceived in your company?" she had just raised her hand and shared that her goal was to be seen as "a good team member."

When I ask this question, it's common for attendees to choose words and speak about roles that feel comfortable for them. Barbara was no different. Although her quiet demeanor, tone of voice, and choice to sit in the back of the room might confirm that a team member goal would be fine for her, I asked if she would be open to the possibility of a bigger goal.

One of my gifts is my ability to create a safe space for people to imagine new possibilities for themselves, especially when they use language filled with clues that tell me they are playing small. I played small too, once upon a time, so I can easily spot my kindred spirits!

This company's culture was positive and diverse, from what I could see, but as a Black woman—and like many other marginalized people—Barbara took a risk by speaking up in a room where she was in the minority. It was risky for her to share how she wanted to be seen in front of a hundred of her peers. Unbeknownst to her, she had taken her first baby step toward becoming more visible and using her voice. She was proud to be viewed as a good team member, but what if she could be more in her career?

A little hesitantly, Barbara agreed to hear the other option I had in mind for her. I knew she had to be curious about what I might say. "What if you changed the goal from being a good team member to being a leader instead?"

The group looked up at me, clearly surprised that I would suggest a much bigger goal, but I saw smiles slowly start to creep across their faces. Although my question was directed to Barbara, I knew others in the room might also need a permission slip to do something bigger with their careers. Their smiles told me that they too were considering the "being a leader" goal.

I let Barbara think about this new option while I told the whole group, "You can be a leader at any level in the company; the title isn't limited to people who lead teams."

I turned back to Barbara and asked, "So how do you feel about changing your goal?" She smiled and said, "It is a much better goal for me!" I watched her demeanor change right before my eyes. She appeared more confident and sat up taller in her chair as she embraced her new vision.

After the session ended, Barbara came up to introduce herself and thanked me for pushing her to view herself differently. She gave me a hug and said, "I can imagine myself as a leader for the first time now!" I could feel her emotion and excitement. All she needed was someone to believe in her. I was so moved by the experience, I almost cried.

Imagine a world where more people were given the chance to play bigger roles and learn how to lead sooner!

I believe that anyone can play a greater leadership role, and that it starts with a shift in their internal beliefs (or the support of someone else who believes in them).

This is the power of helping someone identify new possibilities and move away from their old stories and limiting beliefs. When I talk about playing bigger, so many people have aha moments where they can visualize what is possible for their leadership. They understand how important visibility is to their career success and get excited to try the new ideas we have discussed.

Introduction

My Journey

I refer to Barbara as a kindred spirit because I can relate to playing small in corporate. As an IT director at Kraft, I worked hard and had no idea I wasn't visible enough until a mentor gave me that feedback. It was shocking to me because I had been included in an exclusive leadership program and told I was a top talent; how could I not be visible?

The feedback negatively affected my confidence. I had equated my worth with success in my career, and now my critical inner voice kept saying my career was over. How could I face my mentor and everyone else? Would I need to leave the company? It boiled down to two choices: I could give up the many years I had worked at Kraft and leave, or I could figure out how to be visible in an authentic way. I chose the latter option, having no idea how this one decision would have such a pivotal impact on my life.

The Visibility Factor

Once I made the decision to be visible, everything shifted for me. I experimented with new ways to be visible without bragging and sat at "*the* table" with the executive team. I observed others, adapted new ideas into my own style, and prepared talking points to use when I shared information in conversations and meetings. I knew things had changed when people around the table nodded their heads in agreement. I remained professional and calm on the outside the first time it happened, but on the inside, I was jumping up and down with excitement!

The visibility plan was working, and I knew I couldn't keep it all to myself. Although my team was quieter, focused on performance, and resistant to visibility, I had to teach them what I had learned. What if they could be seen differently too? Although they were hesitant to move out of their comfort zone, they accepted the challenge. They sat at *the* table right next to me and presented to the executive team. It built their confidence. Soon everyone knew who we were, and our bold actions were noticed by our leadership team.

In August 2015, Kraft merged with another consumer product goods company, and I chose to leave. It wasn't an easy decision to leave the company I had been a part of for so many years, but it was time for a new beginning. I started my own coaching and consulting company to help leaders in companies develop their teams, accelerate their own performance, and get positioned for promotions. Deep inside, though, I also wanted to write a book to help leaders learn how to become visible. The problem was, I had no idea how to write or publish a book.

Fortunately, I met AJ Harper, who through her workshop and support helped me write my first book, *The Visibility Factor*. Its core message is that while a leader can work hard, that isn't enough for them to achieve true career success; they need to be visible. Since the book came out in late 2021, my readers have shared the most amazing transformations in how they view themselves, the way they lead, and the opportunities they have gained by being more visible.

I remembered the many conversations I had with readers right after I published *The Visibility Factor*. I was really touched when I heard one of my clients say she loved the book so much, she carried it around in her backpack! She recommended it to many of the people on her team too. Another great moment occurred when I received feedback from an unbiased book reviewer who compared it to Brené Brown's *Dare to Lead*![1] This reviewer had no idea that I had hoped people would compare my book to Brown's books, and it happened! It was a full circle moment for me.

I have also spoken at many companies and led multiple workshops since the book was published. It has been so impactful to observe how people react when they learn about the concept of visibility and realize that they too can be visible. I have seen countless transformations similar to Barbara's happen right before my eyes. Over the last few years, as I met with people through speaking engagements and workshops, they've asked me if I had a workbook to share with them because they were so excited to capture their learnings, delineate their plans, and track their progress. I didn't have anything to fit that need at the time, so I created mini versions of a workbook for them to use.

A Conversation with the Readers

Then I went to a company called Treehouse Foods for a conversation about my book with the Women@Treehouse employee resource group. They had included my book in their book club and were holding the session to meet me and discuss their key takeaways. I walked into the conference room and saw a beautiful bouquet of pink tulips in a clear vase as a gift for me, along with multiple copies of my book for me to sign. Looking back at me from the walls were pictures of inspirational women who have driven visible change: Ruth Bader Ginsburg, Greta Thunberg, Amelia Earhart, and Malala Yousafzai. It felt fitting.

Authors don't always get direct feedback from readers, so I was excited to meet them in person and hear their comments, and honored to be a part of the conversation. Although my book had been featured in other book clubs, this was my first time being in the room for a book club discussion. One woman brought in her copy of the book with at least twenty-five pages marked for reference with Post-it flags. I do the same thing when I read. Holding my book with all her flags in it was surreal.

In *The Visibility Factor*, I share a four-step process for building visibility that I call RISE (reflect, ideate, select, evaluate). The group asked a lot of great questions about how I created RISE, and I shared behind-the-scenes info about some of the stories and situations in the book. This event was so much fun! I would have conversations like this with readers every day if I could!

As we talked, it became clear that, while they had learned the basic concept of visibility and why it was important, there were additional areas where they still needed help. I discovered that although they went through the RISE process, they chose to simply implement some ideas from the book instead of making individual visibility plans. This approach did help them, but they struggled to stay consistent with new actions. To get the results they wanted and reach the next level of visibility, they needed more how-tos.

To achieve real transformation, you need to act consistently. Tracking what you will do and how you will do it means creating a way to capture your plan. I want my readers to be successful, so I asked the group what else would be most helpful for them. Various answers emerged: templates for the visibility plan, ways to track progress, more scripts to follow and examples from real life scenarios, and tools for reframing communication and speaking more powerfully about themselves and their accomplishments.

I said, "If I put all of this into a workbook, would that work?" I saw their faces light up with excitement! They all agreed a workbook would be great. I took their requests plus others from my clients and built a workbook for you too.

Self-Belief

Whether I am coaching individually or speaking to a group, a consistent theme is woven through every visibility conversation: Fear is the major reason for inaction. It feels safer to believe fear-based thoughts, play small, and hide than be in the spotlight and make a mistake in front of others. I used to feel the same way.

When you believe a negative comment, bad experience, or critical message is true, it becomes part of how you see yourself. Let me share something you may not know, though: It doesn't have to be a permanent part of you. You can let go of the limiting belief at any time. Isn't that amazing? When I learned this, it was so empowering for me.

You can simply create a positive belief to replace it. A quick example of a limiting belief: "I am not creative." Thanks to my friend Susie deVille, the author of *Buoyant* who taught me that everyone can be creative, I let go of that old story I had lived with my whole life. My new belief

Introduction

is, "I am creative, and when I write or make art it brings me joy." I now think it's fun to try new things like paint, color, draw, or write a story.

It is a choice to change what you believe. And yes, you will need to reinforce the new belief. You can make this change and see yourself differently right now!

When I first asked my clients for feedback on my coaching, I expected them to say "I learned how to be visible." What I didn't expect was "You helped me believe in myself again." We believe in ourselves at the beginning of our lives; later, when we begin to believe what others say about us, it affects how we see ourselves. I tell clients to build an invisible forcefield around themselves. They get to decide if they want to let anything negative or devaluing come into their world. Acceptance of negative beliefs doesn't have to be an automatic. It too is a choice.

Though I may not coach you directly, my goal is to give you as much support as possible in this workbook so you can absorb and apply its principles quickly. Take your time to process what you are learning and let it sink in. Part of your success will come when you unravel old habits and let go of outdated ideas about your identity. This isn't something that changes overnight, but every minute you put in will pay you back tenfold later on.

Don't give up on this journey. You can do this; all you need to do is take the first step. I believe in you. Like me and my team at Kraft, you have a choice to step out of your comfort zone and try something new. My approach may make you a bit uncomfortable, but I won't ask you to bungee jump (although I have done it, and it was incredible!). This approach will help you grow and offer you the support you need as you let go of the old fear-based messaging that holds you back, take consistent action to build confidence, and stop comparing yourself to others and trust yourself instead. I am here for you as your coach as you make the same journey that I and my clients have been on. This workbook has everything you need to take a new, more visible path!

I want to reassure you of a few things from the start. You are born worthy, and you are amazing. You bring unique strengths to your work, and it isn't your fault that you haven't yet learned what I am sharing with you. I have worked with hundreds of leaders who have also experienced self-doubt. I have observed them question their abilities at the beginning of our coaching relationship and, by the end, come to a place where they trust themselves and feel confident enough to take on whatever they want in their careers. You can experience this too!

You chose this specific workbook for a reason. It spoke to you and what you need. Deep inside, you are ready to solve this challenge. Many years ago, when I searched for ways to become more visible, I couldn't find a book to help me. That's why I wrote *The Visibility Factor* and now this workbook, which provides you with information and activities to help you make a bigger shift. You will be ahead of most people, who don't understand the importance of visibility and how it helps accelerate their careers.

The Visibility Factor is an all-inclusive guide to visibility. This workbook takes you to another level of understanding and application while also providing the foundational elements from the book. The process and activities included in the workbook are exactly what I have used in one-on-one coaching sessions and in workshops.

A CLIENT'S STORY ABOUT SHOWING VALUE

Michelle came to work with me about seven months ago. She said, "I am nervous to take on this new position at a big company and I am not sure how to perform well in this type of culture." Although Michelle had the skills and knowledge to succeed, she also had impostor syndrome. She wasn't sure she could be effective and confident in a complex corporate environment and had some interesting interpersonal dynamics to navigate. She also struggled to be visible in previous roles and wanted to improve her performance. When she second-guessed herself, she chose to stay silent.

We identified her limiting beliefs, and I encouraged her to believe that her voice mattered and to trust herself during challenging conversations and political situations in her company. I asked her to share the conversations she had with clients so I could hear the interactions, understand what was said, reframe situations for her, and help her change her language to demonstrate confidence in upcoming meetings. (You will hear more about the conversations where everything shifted for her in Chapter 6.) As she gained confidence and self-trust, she spoke up instead of letting old patterns hold her back.

At the end of our coaching engagement, I asked her to fill out a feedback form to share what was different for her vs. where she started, and she wrote, "It was great to know there was someone knowledgeable in my corner with whom I could sort out whatever came up. You challenged me to reframe my thinking on situations that I saw in a particular way but for which you saw different possibilities. You helped me find new ways of saying things that showed my value and increased my ability to reflect on what's going on and observe things from different angles. I have increased my confidence that I can be effective in my new environment and that I have something valuable to contribute to the company."

Michelle learned how to show her value and stand out amongst her peers. An unexpected reorganization happened at her company recently and, though she had been there less than a year, she was offered her choice of three different roles. If she had not focused on showing her value, as a newer hire, they could easily have let her go instead.

Opportunities are offered to so many of my clients when they learn how to show up with full ownership of their value and demonstrate their capabilities. You can have this experience too.

Workbook Structure

This workbook will guide you on a journey to greater visibility through the exploration of five key steps and an important question to answer at each step. In Part 1, you will focus on the first three steps. In Part 2, you will take a break to review the Foundations for Success, which provide you with the information you need for the final two steps at the beginning of Part 3. Once you complete the last two steps, you can focus on the solutions and actions that will help you achieve greater visibility!

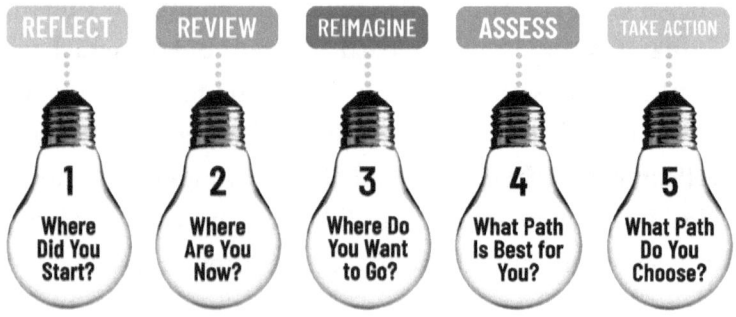

Figure I.1: 5 Steps to Greater Visibility

Here are a few more details about the three parts of the workbook:

PART 1—VISIBILITY AND CAREER GROWTH FRAMEWORK

This includes the following three steps:

- **Chapter 1: Reflect** – Where did you start?
- **Chapter 2: Review** – Where are you now?
- **Chapter 3: Reimagine** – Where do you want to go?

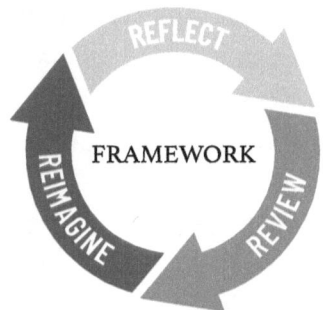

Figure I.2: Visibility and Career Growth Framework

In these chapters, I will guide you as you **reflect** on the beginning of your career to gain new insights about yourself, identify patterns, and remember experiences that you may have forgotten. Next, you will **review** where you are in your career today to determine if you are where you want to be. The important last step is to **reimagine** your future career.

PART 2 – FOUNDATIONS FOR SUCCESS

In Part 2, "Foundations for Success," you will pause to learn some of the key concepts from *The Visibility Factor* and additional, essential information about personal brand, value, and confidence. These foundations will support you on your journey.

- **Core Foundations** – This section delves into what visibility is, why it is important, and what holds you back from standing out. (You may be tempted to skip this chapter if you have read the book, but I have included new exercises and information here that you won't want to miss.)

- **Personal Branding Foundation** – This foundation illuminates your current brand and perception, helps you define your new narrative, and guides you through the creation of personal brand messaging that will help you become more visible.
- **Showing Value and Building Confidence Foundation** – This foundation helps you recognize your value and trust yourself to take bigger actions, demonstrating confidence to decision-makers who can recommend you for new opportunities.

PART 3 – ASSESS CHALLENGES AND TAKE ACTION

Once you have completed the Visibility and Career Growth Framework and the Foundations for Success, you will have what you need to continue on the journey and take the last two steps to answer the final two questions. The answers you come up with will lead you to solution paths that offer new techniques and ideas for increasing your visibility.

- Chapter 7 provides a visibility challenge self-assessment to determine what challenges impact you most. I group these challenges into three categories: communication/clarity, influence/relationships, and leadership/being strategic.
- Chapter 8 explains the three solution paths (each of which is aligned with a challenge path) to support you with the challenges you identified in Chapter 7.
- Chapters 9 through 11 are dedicated to the three solution paths. You can start by exploring your primary path, which you will identify through the assessment in Chapter 7, or take a "choose your own adventure" approach. I loved those books when I was a kid!

Choose Your Own Adventure

I love to travel and create new experiences, but most of the time I don't view myself as the adventurous type. Traveling to unfamiliar places

Introduction

stresses me out. Most people would never guess this about me, but when I go somewhere new, I tend to feel anxious. It is just uncertainty about traveling there for the first time; it is temporary. I am fine once I get where I am going and always so happy I went! I recognize this pattern of mine now. While I acknowledge that there will be some uncertainty, instead of letting it hold me back, I channel it into excitement about experiencing the new place and meeting new people.

My friend Sheri is my opposite when it comes to travel. She is brave and loves to go to new places whenever the opportunity arises. She and her family have traveled all over the world and been to places that are out of my comfort zone. Sheri and her husband have created so many priceless memories as a family. For example, they are about to take a "mystery vacation." This is a guided trip and all they have is a packing list, a travel date, and a time to show up at the airport to fly off on their adventure. What? They will only find out where they are going twenty-four hours before they leave. So much uncertainty is not my style, but I love how excited they are to take this trip together. They are setting an example for their kids, teaching them to explore the world and enjoy the adventure!

The choose-your-own-adventure approach allows you to select the type of experience that works best for you. You have everything you need already, so there is no packing required. You will tap into your experiences, beliefs, assumptions, and challenges as you travel. The goal is to help you view your career from a different perspective and identify what led you to this moment. You will journey back in time, view where you are currently, and then create the future. The workbook and ideas will be here for you whenever you need them.

Are you excited to begin? I hope you are! Whether you are similar to Sheri or more like me, you will learn so much about yourself throughout this journey. By the end, you will be transformed.

This workbook will guide you on a fun adventure as you learn more about yourself and choose your path. I will be in your corner supporting you, as I did with Michelle, and you will have access to all the stories, resources, templates, and frameworks you need for the journey. Now, you may be similar to Sheri and can't wait to start the adventure, but I ask you to go through the exercises in each chapter in order. That order is intentionally designed to help you slow down and experience the insights that will be most meaningful for you. If you need more room for your answers as you write, you can use a notebook or capture your answers digitally.

If you complete this workbook, you can expect to:

- Understand what visibility is and why it is important for career success.
- Think differently about visibility and identify new possibilities for your leadership.
- Identify your limiting beliefs and fears so you can shift them.
- Create a new narrative about yourself to share with others.
- Understand impostor syndrome and how to manage it.
- Create a plan to execute so others will see your value.
- Reflect more deeply on your career and who you are as a leader.
- Communicate your values and influence others to help you maximize your potential.
- Understand more about your personal brand and build your confidence.

Here is my promise to you: I will give you the process, tools, and resources to help you move from overlooked and invisible to confident, valued, visible, and positioned for the opportunities you want in your career. Let's go!

PART 1
VISIBILITY AND CAREER GROWTH FRAMEWORK

The three-step framework for reflecting upon, reviewing, and reimagining your career growth through a lens of visibility, value, and influence.

Chapter 1
STEP 1: REFLECT—WHERE DID YOU START?

Inside Chapter 1

So much of what you learned and experienced at the start of your career stays with you and becomes a part of you. Though we don't always take the time for this kind of reflection, understanding why we do what we do and how it started is important. The following exercises will help you explore the first step on your journey to greater visibility—reflecting on, "Where did you start?" When you finish this chapter, you will view your past with fresh eyes.

Growing Up

When I was young, I wanted to be a kindergarten or second-grade teacher. It was perfect for me: I could write on the chalkboard, read books, color, and teach kids all day long. Looking back now, I think it was because I loved my kindergarten and second-grade teachers. They were kind and created a fun learning experience. (I left out first grade because of the first-grade teacher. She was cranky and mean.)

As I got older, I watched my mom leave for work in a suit and fly to New York and Florida. I didn't totally understand what she did, but it appeared to be a great job, seemed fun, and I admired her success so much that business became an area of interest for me. We may have an idea of what we want to do for a career when we are kids but then be influenced by others over time. I considered business over teaching simply because my mom showed me a different option.

We are heavily influenced by our families, friends, schools, and social and mainstream media to choose a "good" career. You might hear that you should choose a certain career because it makes more money or offers more perks. Or you might be pressured to follow in the footsteps of family members and become a doctor, lawyer, or business owner. Where you end up could be the complete opposite of what you imagined when you were a child and have little to do with your degree or your strengths.

I wanted to go into psychology in college but talked myself out of it. I ended up going into business (Mom influence) and graduated with degrees in marketing and production management. My roles at Kraft in sales, supply chain, and information technology had little to do with my degrees. Here is the interesting part, though. I took neither the teaching nor the psychology path, but as a coach, I teach and use psychology principles with clients all the time. It's fascinating how things work out, isn't it? The path I chose was an even better one for me. I got to bring business, teaching, and psychology together in my role as a coach.

Let's explore what you wanted to do as you progressed into the work world. Do you have a similar story to mine?

CHILDHOOD CAREER IDEAS EXERCISE

You were probably asked this question by family members or teachers when you were a child. Do you remember how you answered, "What do you want to be when you grow up?"

Step 1: Reflect—Where Did You Start?

....

....

....

....

....

....

....

Your First Job

My first real adult job out of college was only loosely connected with my management and marketing degrees. My college roommate got me a job doing research for an investor relations company, which showed me the world of institutional investing. I had a ninety-minute commute by car and train, each way, to the office in Chicago. The commute wasn't ideal, but I needed experience on my résumé, and it would only be for ten months. My new employer wasn't aware at the time, but I was getting married and planned to move out of state. Although it wasn't the job I had imagined for myself and I was a bit overwhelmed by how much there was to learn, I soaked up as much knowledge as I could. I learned about the business and how to work with different kinds of people, and I got my first real exposure to computers. I had no idea at the time how much these experiences would prepare me for my future.

Do you remember your first day at your first "real" job? Did you wonder if you had been dropped into a new world? Did it feel like everyone else had the playbook and knew how to operate in the environment while you were a rookie just trying to figure it out? Over time, you learned to adapt to the pace, the work, the culture, and the rules in order to succeed in the company.

FIRST JOB EXERCISE

What was your first job as an adult, and what were your responsibilities? (If you had a summer or other job in high school or an internship that taught you a lot, write that down instead.)

....

....

....

....

....

....

FIRST JOB LEARNINGS EXERCISE

What was your first real job experience like for you? (What did it teach you? Did you have a good boss? Did you enjoy the work?)

....

....

....

....

....

....

Step 1: Reflect—Where Did You Start?

Your first job experience shapes you as a person and future leader in so many ways. When you join a company, you are the new person who wants to fit in quickly. Every day, you learn new things and acclimate further to the culture, the work, and the people. As you gain knowledge and observe what others are doing, you create work habits that become part of your foundation for the future. You learn how to get tasks done, manage your time, build relationships, communicate, solve problems, ask questions, and work with a team. Hopefully, you also learn how to have a working relationship with your manager to ensure that you get feedback, learn essential information, and align for your career progression.

FIRST JOB REFLECTION EXERCISE

What did you take away from your first role? Did you learn any rules, beliefs, or behaviors that you still use now? (For example, do you never question your manager? Do you believe that you must take a role when it is offered or you might not get any more offers?)

....

....

....

....

....

....

....

....

Part 1: Visibility and Career Growth Framework

Pivotal Moments

"The witch is on her broom…"

In the movie *The Proposal*, set in the office of Colden Books Publishing company, this instant message is sent to the whole department by Ryan Reynolds, who plays the assistant to the editor-in-chief. His boss, played by Sandra Bullock, is about to walk into the office, and his message is a warning to appear busy or deal with the consequences. After the office staff receives it, the scene shifts from a friendly group of people having conversations and their morning coffee to a stressed-out group of people hiding in their cubicles to avoid her wrath and criticism.[2] Replace Sandra Bullock with my first CEO and it is the exact scene my co-workers and I experienced every morning at my first job.

Unfortunately, we didn't have instant messaging in that job; I wish we had. Some of my co-workers and I sat in the back of the office, and our only warning was when we heard the CEO's loud, booming voice barking orders. He was a former Navy man from the East Coast, shorter in stature, and had a strong vision for the company he was building. He was smart and well regarded for the innovations he created in the investor relations field, but although he had a strong reputation externally, it was chaotic within the walls of our twelve-person company. He would pit people against each other and changed his mind a lot, which made it more difficult to get things done.

This office environment didn't compare to any workplace I had been in before. I had visited the office at General Foods where my mom worked many times and never seen anyone yell at people. However, when it is your company, you can do what you want. This man was the CEO and owner and ran the company as if he was still in the military. You were expected to follow orders or deal with the consequences. I immediately got a pit in my stomach when he started hollering at people and didn't want to experience the wrath he inflicted on others, so I avoided him. The five-foot cubicle wall divider between my desk and my co-worker's provided some protection.

Step 1: Reflect—Where Did You Start?

As I mentioned earlier, my preferred approach was to blend in, get along, keep my mouth shut, and do my work. In other words, I played small, people-pleased, didn't challenge, and focused only on my performance to avoid conflict. Can you see how I adopted those behaviors to protect myself? I was still doing those same things when I got the feedback from my mentor about my lack of visibility. All those years later it was still impacting me, and I had no idea I was doing it. This is why reflection is so important and can have such a big effect.

A postscript to this story: I recently found my old CEO's obituary online and gained some new insight into why he may have acted the way he did all those years ago. He was struggling with things I didn't know about that explained his behavior. What he did to us was not okay, but people act in certain ways because of how they think about themselves. I think he put a ton of pressure on himself—and projected it onto his team—to prove his value to the external community. I didn't understand or respect him as a twenty-one-year-old first-time employee, but I can have compassion and forgive him as an adult and coach.

Silver linings can always be found later, when you review the past, but they are hard to recognize when you are in the midst of a difficult experience. Reflection helps you process any situation, good or bad, with a new perspective. It also gives you the opportunity to move on. I hope my example with my first boss helps you see what is possible.

As I worked on this chapter and took myself back in time to write about my first job, I realized I'd had no idea then how toxic the culture was and the impact it had on me. I was so young when I started there and had never been around anyone who verbally abused people; I think it was easier for me to block it out.

Blending in, getting along, and keeping my mouth shut wasn't a recipe to stand out and be visible, was it? When people struggle with visibility, the reasons are usually driven by fear, past experiences, or insecurity.

That first job was a difficult environment, and the immediate stress response the boss's tirades created in me deeply affected my ability to speak up. I remove myself from such situations now, but as a young woman who didn't want to fail, I didn't have the power or confidence to do it then. The power of reflecting on old situations is in discovering what you couldn't recognize before due to the growth you have experienced since. Reflection is the first step toward letting go of old beliefs and achieving what you want.

PIVOTAL MOMENTS EXERCISE

What pivotal or difficult moments have stayed with you from your first job? How did they change you and create beliefs, assumptions, or doubts that you are still holding onto?

....

....

....

....

....

....

....

....

....

....

....

....

Step 1: Reflect—Where Did You Start?

When you hold onto a negative view of yourself, it will be difficult for you to be visible until you do the work to change it. Once you are aware of the limiting belief, create a new positive belief to replace it. Otherwise, you will continue to operate through the lens of the old belief and prevent yourself from living up to your potential. You will continue to unconsciously self-sabotage to stay safe and keep those beliefs and assumptions intact. I did this to myself, and my clients have done it to themselves too. This may be your first time learning about this, but now you know. Stay open and reflect on your own experiences so you can shift when necessary.

Key Takeaways

I hope this journey down memory lane has given you some new insights. What did you learn early in your career that impacted you and is still a challenge? What did you learn by taking this first step and reflecting on, "Where did you start?" that will help you achieve greater visibility?

....

....

....

....

....

....

....

....

....

Part 1: Visibility and Career Growth Framework

Chapter 2
STEP 2: REVIEW—WHERE ARE YOU NOW?

Inside Chapter 2

In Chapter 1, you reflected on learnings from your early career. Now it is time to move into the present and explore your current state. The objective is to have you consider where you are in your career right now and help you gain clarity for the future. The following exercises will help you explore the second step on your journey to greater visibility as you review: "Where are you now?"

TERESA'S STORY

The first time I met Teresa, I noticed she had a quieter personality, but when she spoke, I could tell she had thick skin and wasn't afraid to challenge someone when things were wrong. She talked about the roles she'd had throughout her tenure at her company, her struggles, and what she liked to do outside of work. She loved what she was working on at the time and was making measurable improvements. Teresa traveled a lot in her role and smiled when she shared the feedback from teams at the sites. She was proud of her accomplishments and these teams clearly respected her knowledge and experience.

When I asked her to share her goals for our coaching time together, her whole demeanor changed. "My biggest issue is how my site leader treats me. I am so frustrated with him. I am going to give him a piece of mind as soon as we are off this call." She was clearly stressed. I had no idea what had happened, but I knew that yelling at him wouldn't solve the problem. I slowed way down and asked her to share what had happened to make her so mad. She said, "In a meeting today, I shared an update with a group of my peers and this leader, and in the middle of my update, he cut me off. I tried to explain it to him again, but he didn't want to hear it. He does this to me all the time and I am sick of it. I get feedback from so many other groups that I am doing great work. I don't understand why he does this to me." Teresa's story and the way he dismissed her gave me pause. So many memories rushed back to me. She and I had both had experiences that spoke volumes about how we were undervalued. The disrespectful approach of our leaders had sent us a clear message with long-lasting ramifications: "What you have to say isn't important."

It was clear to me that Teresa would have to take a different approach to conversations with her site leader. I told her that we could move her past this situation and that her manager would soon value her. Her furrowed brow and the way she sat back in her chair told me she was skeptical. I understood that Teresa couldn't imagine what was possible yet, but every person I have ever coached has gone into these challenges resistant at first, unable to see what they can do, and come out the other side as leaders who believe in themselves and their value.

You will hear more about Teresa's story in Chapter 6 and learn the steps she took to work through this situation with her site leader.

Meeting Clients Where They Are

When a new client comes to work with me, I ask them questions, as I did with Teresa, to understand their current situation. I listen to what they are saying while also observing their body language and listening for what they are leaving out. My goal is to build a space of trust for them to share whatever they want so they can get it all off their chest.

In my experience, people hold onto resentments, anger, and negative beliefs for a long time. Here is how this happens: Let's say Bill encounters a difficult situation that brings up negative emotions. He "has no time" for self-reflection or interest in dealing with any of it, so he buries it all inside. Bill tells himself a story to rationalize moving on without actually handling it.

It may feel like the easier decision at the time, but it takes so much energy to hold onto the negative when you could redeploy it in a more positive way. I was a master at doing that for so many years, and had no idea there was another way to manage those situations and emotions. If this is something you have experienced too, you will have to deal with what occurred or your body will force you to deal with it later. Coaching helps clients move through the old stories, feelings, and beliefs they have held onto for a long time so they can learn from them, let them go, and move into new possibilities.

NEW CLIENT EXERCISE

Let's pretend you are a new client of mine. Tell me about your role. What is going well, what are your challenges, and what do you want to be different? (No filtering, just write and get it all out.)

....

....

Part 1: Visibility and Career Growth Framework

....
....
....
....
....
....
....
....
....
....
....
....
....
....

• • • • • • • • • • • • • • • • • • •

SELF-NARRATIVE EXERCISE

How do you describe yourself to others as a leader and in your role? Share whatever comes to mind and what you would normally tell someone.

....
....

Step 2: Review—Where Are You Now?

CO-WORKERS' NARRATIVE ABOUT YOU EXERCISE

A narrative is a story, and other people have narratives about you based on what you have shared with them and their own observations. If people in your organization were asked about you, what do you think they would share about you?

Career Self-Assessment

Let's start with some quick yes or no answers to the below questions to assess your career. Review what you captured about yourself in the last three exercises and circle *Y* for yes or *N* for no to answer each of the questions. Go with your gut reaction.

- Y N Is your career where you want it to be?
- Y N Are you perceived well and on track for the future roles you want?
- Y N Do you enjoy what you do?
- Y N Does your job fulfill you?
- Y N Does it align with your values, priorities, and strengths?
- Y N Do you spend your time on the right things?
- Y N Do you take advantage of opportunities to become more visible?

These questions do not render a simple yes or no answer every time. You might answer yes one day, while on other days the answer might be no. If you honestly answer no to many of the items on the list the majority of the time, I invite you to identify actions you could take to shift those answers to yes. Determine if there are some easy actions you could include in your plan. Perhaps others will require a bigger change. Keep these questions in mind as you go through the rest of the exercises in this chapter and stay open to receiving additional insight.

CAREER SELF-ASSESSMENT REFLECTION EXERCISE

What did you learn by completing the career self-assessment?

....

....

Step 2: Review—Where Are You Now?

Based on the previous exercises and your own career self-assessment, is there anything you want to change? In other words, what do you want the narrative about you to be? (Keep this in mind for the work you will do in Chapter 3.)

I built this assessment to be a quick way of reflecting on your career. You may only reflect on your career progress during your performance review each year. What if you did this type of check-in each quarter instead? Imagine being able to share what you have done, articulate the value you bring, and share where you stand in your career in conversations and in your review.

What Do You Do?

"What do you do?" is a question everyone is asked throughout their careers. I remember being introduced to people and trying to explain what I did in IT. I saw their eyes glaze over as they did their best to understand it, knowing they never would.

Of course, the answer will change as you change jobs and companies, but have you ever given any consideration to how you answer the question? The way you talk about what you do is important, but most people never consider that. Let's dig a little deeper into what you say you do.

NETWORKING EVENT EXERCISE

Imagine you are at a networking event. Someone in the group you are standing by asks you, "So tell me—what you do?" Share what you would normally tell someone in response to the question. Don't overthink it.

....

....

....

....

....

Step 2: Review—Where Are You Now?

NETWORKING EVENT REFLECTION EXERCISE

Go back and read what you wrote in the previous exercise. Review it as objectively as possible. Is the tone positive, negative, or mixed? What messages do your words send others about you, how you see yourself, and your role? This is only for you, so be honest in your reflection below.

Did you find the last two questions challenging to answer? You might simply have responded to the networking exercise with your title and company name, or maybe you used a lot of detail. This deeper review is what will help you gain clarity about where you are now. Let's try out a few more exercises to help you reflect on your leadership and your career.

Unique Gifts

"There is nothing that makes me unique."

This is a common response from clients to my question, "What is unique about you?" Everyone has unique gifts that enable them to stand out from others, but those gifts aren't always recognized as valuable by the person who has them. They may come in the form of skills, experiences, or natural abilities. Clients can't recognize the value of these gifts because they come so easily and therefore seem unimportant and inconsequential. Somehow, they got the message that only the hard things are valuable. Instead of celebrating their gifts, they hide, diminish, and downplay them so that others aren't threatened by them and they can avoid judgment and criticism. Clients are always amazed at the results of this next exercise and surprised by how much they have to offer. It is time for the message to change. Let's bring out those unique gifts to show your value!

WHAT MAKES YOU UNIQUE? EXERCISE - PART 1

What makes you unique? (Think about your roles, business and industry experience, where you have lived, your strengths, talents, etc.)

....

....

....

Step 2: Review—Where Are You Now?

WHAT MAKES YOU UNIQUE? EXERCISE - PART 2

Now pretend you are in an interview situation. What would you say to highlight what makes you unique so you will stand out against other candidates?

_____

_____

_____

_____

_____

Have you been reluctant to bring up what makes you unique for fear of being viewed as a braggart? How about things you've done that others have no idea about because you haven't brought them up?

What was different for you when I asked you to imagine yourself in an interview situation? It forced you to identify what makes you stand out in consideration for the pretend job. Yet you aren't embracing those qualities to help you stand out in your current role. Slow down and reflect on the reasons why you are hiding your gifts.

You have a choice: Be the person who devalues what makes you great, or the person who embraces your unique gifts to help you stand out, make an impact, and add value.

Are You Ready For The Future?

Before we go on to the next chapter to explore the future, we will take a brief pause. I want to acknowledge the effort you've put into self-discovery during these first two chapters. It isn't easy to review your past to discern what happened and assign meaning to it. In my experience, reflection is something few leaders do. A review of where you are right now isn't easy, either. You may believe you haven't accomplished enough yet. Self-judgment and self-criticism may show up if you aren't quite where you want to be. Those self-imposed expectations raise anxiety and fear within you, causing you to stop expecting and aiming for the career you once hoped for.

Step 2: Review—Where Are You Now?

What if I asked you to look at this in a new way? What if everything you have done so far is exactly what you needed to do in preparation for a future role? Does that change the way you view your progress up till now? Each career experience gave you gifts, and now you get to keep what serves you and let the rest go.

This reflection work has prepared you for what comes next. If you want to make big shifts as you focus on the future, you will need to bring out a new side of yourself. What if we try out the word "bold" to describe you? Being bold has a powerful connotation and you might resist at first, but let's just experiment and call you a bold leader. You are trying on this new identity for a moment. Let's explore the possibility of what being a bold leader might mean for you!

What if being bold helped you reach a role that is bigger than you had imagined? Imagine for a moment that you are a top talent and people want to work for you and learn from you. What if calling yourself a bold leader shifted your view and helped you believe in new possibilities? Sometimes it can be just that simple.

Let me share a story of someone who would never have used the word "bold" to describe herself before we worked together to create her visibility plan.

AMELIA'S STORY

Amelia had been in her role at her company for fifteen years when we started coaching together. She did well in her department and in her quiet way, she was innovative. Amelia was intelligent, and also an introvert who struggled to communicate what she was doing and why it mattered. Others perceived that she was a hard worker, and reserved, but she wasn't viewed as a leader.

Amelia had a fire inside of her that no one at her company understood. Though she had asked to do something else, everyone assumed she was fine staying where she was and couldn't imagine her in a leadership role. They dismissed her and made assumptions about her. Unfortunately, this is a common occurrence when a leader doesn't have clarity about what they want to do and isn't sure how to talk about the value they could bring to another role. When we started coaching, Amelia told me her whole story. She knew she could do well in a new role if given the chance.

She said, "I have tried so many approaches to talk about what I want, but nothing works. I just don't know what to do." I saw how dejected she was, and that she feared nothing would ever change. I gave her a moment before I quietly said, "Are you ready to try something different? Are you willing to trust me and try a new approach?" She looked up at me and I saw a little bit of hope in her expression. I said, "This will take work, and you will need to be bold and try things that are out of your comfort zone. This is a journey to increase your visibility. It won't happen overnight, but I will be there to coach you through it."

From that moment on, Amelia dedicated herself to the visibility plan she had created. We talked about whom she needed to meet, whom she could ask to be her mentor, and what she would discuss in those conversations. She wasted no time. By our next meeting, she had reached out to multiple VPs in her company as well as HR, and gotten meetings on the calendar with them. We focused on her communication, confidence, and how she could clearly share what she wanted and ask for support to help her get there. At each coaching session, she shared updates on the conversations she'd had and the new people she had connected with during the week, and we strategized for her next meetings. She continued to add people to meet with and we prepared her for those conversations too.

Step 2: Review—Where Are You Now?

> In one of our last sessions together, I told her how I saw her confidence grow during our time together and how brilliantly she had executed her visibility plan. I asked her what shifted for her during coaching. Her feedback to me was, "You have helped me go from someone who was unknown to boldly connecting with senior leaders and asking for what I want." I loved hearing her say those words. She was showing up in a much bolder way.

In the next chapter, you will start to focus on where you want to go next. What could you accomplish and who could you be as a bolder leader? Your visibility journey can include possibilities that didn't exist for you before! You can take actions that will make you feel brave and bold, boosting your confidence. Others will notice and recognize that you are ready for a bigger role!

Key Takeaways

What are your key takeaways to act on, based on where you are in your career right now? Do you recognize any patterns in the way you describe your work and yourself? What did you learn from Step 2 as you answered, "Where are you now?" that will help you achieve greater visibility?

....

....

....

....

....

Part 1: Visibility and Career Growth Framework

Chapter 3
STEP 3: REIMAGINE—WHERE DO YOU WANT TO GO?

Inside Chapter 3

The objective of this chapter is to help you figure out where you want to be in the future. This is a big question, and it may not be easy for you to make this decision, so let's explore your various career possibilities. I have included tools here that will help you find clarity, identify an outcome, and establish who you need to be to achieve it. Let's take Step 3 and answer the third question on your journey to greater visibility as you reimagine: "Where do you want to go?"

Choose Your Own Adventure

If you don't take charge of your career, someone else will.

My corporate career isn't something I took charge of at all throughout my twenty-six years with my company. If I am honest, Kraft steered it through all its twists and turns. Don't get me wrong, I had a great career there in many ways by being a part of four different functions of the company. When I came up through the organization, the culture and messaging were pretty simple. You couldn't say no to the opportunities offered you or you risked being excluded from future discussions for roles. Employees who wanted to get ahead did what was best for the company, and I was a loyal Kraft girl. Some of those roles made no sense for me based on my education and experience, but I figured them out and learned so much in those uncomfortable situations.

I had what is known as an accidental career. This happens when you lack clarity on what you want in your career, default to the role you are given, work hard and hope you are noticed, and are too busy to focus on anything but your job. I lacked intention, didn't communicate what I wanted, and assumed my work would speak for itself. I have no regrets, though. I learned a lot through those experiences and those lessons still serve me today. However, I have often wondered what my life would have been like if I had intentionally chosen a path.

As Maya Angelou said, "Do the best you can until you know better. Then when you know better, do better."[3]

I want my clients to understand that they can proactively drive their careers too. Knowing what to do and doing it are two different things. Figuring out the next step in your career can be a challenge. Is it a challenge for you too? It is a big decision, and no one wants to make the wrong one. Life comes with no guarantees. You need to know the next destination, but it doesn't have to be the final one. It is important to find clarity and trust yourself to make the best decision in the moment. Again, your next move doesn't need to be permanent. The two tools below will help you gain additional insight as you consider your future.

The Career Clarity Framework

When I was growing up, you could only imagine a future career based on what the people around you did for work. In fact, according to a recent article, "During the 1970s and 1980s, careers were often characterized by long-term employment with a single company. Job security was the most important factor with most people staying in jobs for life. Professionals typically specialized in a specific field or role, with clear, hierarchical progression paths and didn't divert off it."

This long-term employment meant you didn't have to explore new careers. Once you got the job, you stayed until retirement. The article highlights some of the major changes that have taken place over the

Step 3: Reimagine—Where Do You Want to Go?

last forty or so years: "the digital age, dot coms, the internet, the gig economy and remote work."[4] Each of these changes had a tremendous impact on the evolution of companies, jobs, and what is now possible for you in your career. Change brings opportunities, but when there are so many choices, it can be overwhelming.

I created the Career Clarity Framework to help leaders evaluate roles against their own priorities. You need to know what you want in your career in order to communicate it. For example, if your manager asks you what you want to do next, will you have a ready answer? Many of the people I have coached said no, at first. Without clarity, there are too many choices to pick from, and without a plan to follow to get to a decision, they shut down. This is usually the time when they come to me for help and I get to show them a better way.

Three categories are included in the Career Clarity Framework: needs, nice-to-haves, and deal-breakers. I have a favorite analogy for helping clients understand the framework the first time they use it: Let's pretend you are searching for a new place to live. Use the three categories in the framework to figure out what you truly need and want.

- What does your new house or apartment need to have for you to say yes to buying or renting it? (For example, the number of bedrooms, number of bathrooms, a garage, etc.)
- What are the "nice-to-haves" that the house or apartment might include? (Like a basement, gym, fenced yard, etc.)
- Finally, what are the deal-breakers (For example, price higher than budget, extra fees, location too far from work, etc.)?

Defining what is important to you is what brings clarity and allows you to make decisions more objectively and with less emotion. To elaborate on this example, let's apply it to the framework.

- Step one is to complete the framework before you start looking for places to live.

- You find three great apartments to choose from. Compare what they offer to what you defined in your framework.
- If your favorite apartment of the three is $2,100 and you listed rent higher than $1,800 as a deal-breaker, you have to decide if you will stick with your original limit or not.

Falling in love with a great apartment is easy to do. The framework doesn't take away your choices; it simply allows you to slow down and make a *conscious* choice so that you don't regret it later.

CLARITY ABOUT YOUR NEXT ROLE EXERCISE

Now let's leverage the Career Clarity Framework for your future role. Here is an example to give you some ideas before you complete your own.

NEED TO HAVE IN NEXT ROLE	NICE TO HAVE IN NEXT ROLE	DEAL-BREAKER
People management	Remote work opportunity	Moving to a new location
Decision-making authority	Vendor management	75% or more travel
Opportunity to lead a global initiative	Large team	No opportunity for further advancement
Senior manager or higher level of responsibility	Client-facing Role	Not a visible role

Figure 3.1: Career Clarity Framework

Here are some things to consider as you fill out your framework:

- What did you enjoy or dislike in past roles?

Step 3: Reimagine—Where Do You Want to Go?

- What are your strengths?
- What gaps do you have in skills, experience and/or education that might hold you back from future roles?
- What brings you joy?
- What would make you feel excited to get up in the morning?
- What are your priorities in life right now?

You don't have to fill in all the boxes if you don't want to, and I included extra space if you need it. This is your framework to use in whatever way it helps you, and you can update it throughout your career.

NEED TO HAVE IN NEXT ROLE	NICE TO HAVE IN NEXT ROLE	DEAL-BREAKER

Part 1: Visibility and Career Growth Framework

What clarity do you have after completing the framework?

....
....
....
....
....
....

What else might you need to do to gain further clarity? (For example, meet with people who are currently in the role, get advice from a mentor, or do some job shadowing?)

....
....
....
....
....
....
....

You Have a Choice

Let's slow down and check in on where you are in this journey: You reflected on your past experiences to decide what they mean to you and

Step 3: Reimagine—Where Do You Want to Go?

what you learned. Then you spent some time reviewing where you are now and identifying what makes you valuable and unique. If you went through the exercises too fast and had no takeaways, you need to go back and review before you continue.

What new perspectives have you gained to use as you create your future? You can't change what has occurred in your career up until now, but you can learn from it and be intentional with what you want going forward. I am a big believer in letting clients decide. They always have a choice. I want you to feel the same agency in making your own decisions.

CHOOSE YOUR NEXT STEP EXERCISE

When someone considers a career transition, there are generally four different options to choose from. To keep it simple, I've listed them here along with some questions to review for each.

- **Take a new role in your company:** Do you have a role in mind? Is there a next logical step for you in the company? What do you hope to gain in a new role?
- **Stay where you are and don't make a change:** What happens if you do nothing?
- **Leave your company:** Would a new company and role help you develop more skills, give you a new experience, and/or offer you a promotion or better compensation?
- **Choose to do something totally different that is meant for you:** Do you have a bigger purpose?

It seems as if it was just yesterday when I pondered these four options. I was a little discombobulated (my grandma's favorite word) on the first day after I left Kraft Heinz. One day I had a crazy schedule of meetings and important work to do, and the next, I had nothing to do. I decided to go for a walk in a park near my house after I dropped the kids off at school. It was a bright, sunny morning and the park had a nice walking path shaded by some beautiful trees. As I walked the path, I said to myself, *Well, Sue, it seems as if you have four options to consider.*

Here is what came up for me as I pondered them:

- **Take a new role in your company:** I could potentially take another role at the company if one became available, but I knew it would not fulfill me and that it was time to move on.
- **Stay where you are and make no change:** I didn't have the option to keep my role with the same responsibilities. I left because my job was going to change a lot, and the company was shifting priorities to focus on areas I wasn't as passionate about or motivated to work on.
- **Leave your company:** I could take another IT role in another company, but I was burned out by corporate and needed a break.
- **Choose to do something totally different that is meant for you:** I could start my own coaching and consulting company and make a bigger impact than I could at Kraft. (I had already completed my coaching certification. It was my plan B for someday and this situation accelerated my plan to move ahead sooner than expected.)

I went through these options in my head and knew the choice I needed to pick was the one that scared me the most. It was not an easy decision to walk away from a secure company where I had been for so many years. Starting my own company to help people become visible leaders was exciting for me, but it was also scary. I had never started a business before. I was leaving the company I loved, letting go of friends and colleagues, and giving up a steady paycheck. Heading out into the unknown to start something new was risky.

Review the following to confirm if staying where you are is the best choice right now and take notes. What are your answers for each option?

Step 3: Reimagine—Where Do You Want to Go?

Take a new role in your company:

....

....

Stay where you are and make no change:

....

....

Leave your company:

....

....

Choose to do something totally different that is meant for you:

....

....

What choice will you make?

....

....

....

....

....

Mindset Comes First

When you choose the next step, it is important to consider how you view yourself right now. Why? No change can be made until you think the thought and decide. Once you decide, the actions to make it happen will follow. Here is an excerpt from *The Visibility Factor* on this topic: "I have always battled with the stories I told myself. I didn't understand how thoughts worked, so to me it was just my reality. My struggles make sense now, because I have learned that thoughts drive behaviors and actions. I didn't question my thoughts, and I underestimated how powerful thoughts and the stories you tell yourself can be. They can either help you move forward or keep you stuck in place."

Remember Barbara, from the introduction? She was keeping herself small until I challenged her to reframe her capabilities and leadership. Barbara is just one example of many clients and workshop participants who have gone through this deceptively simple exercise but found it to be one of the most powerful. You need to understand where you are now and *then* take the next step.

. . . .

CURRENT LEADERSHIP VIEW EXERCISE:

Now it is your turn. Use what you have learned in Chapters 1 and 2 as you review where you are today. Do you remember when I asked you to create a self-narrative in Chapter 2? What was your response? Write it out again here.

....

....

....

....

Step 3: Reimagine—Where Do You Want to Go?

....
....
....
....

What key words did you include in your narrative? Use any of those words and add any others you wish to complete the template below. Fill in the blanks to generate a sentence that describes who you are now. If you want to adjust the sentence structure below a bit you can, but the goal is to come up with one sentence that shows who you are right now. Here is an example from Sarah, a client of mine:

I am a(n) __*empathetic*__ , __*kind*__ (2 adjectives) leader who __*uses*__ (verb) __*creativity*__ (strength), and __*relationships*__ (strength) to __*solve*__ (verb) __*problems of all sizes for the organization*__ (outcome).

I am a(n) _____ , _____ (2 adjectives) leader who _____ (verb) _____ (strength), and _____ (strength) to _____ (verb) _____ (outcome).

Write your current leadership view from the completed template in the space below. Does it reflect who you are today? If not, change the words to better align with your style. If you like, you can simplify or adjust this statement to make it flow better.

....

....

....

....

....

....

....

Create the Future

Now that you have articulated who you are today, you need to create a similar statement for the future you that you aspire to be. I ask a question of many clients when they are trying to move into a bigger role or take on a lot more responsibility: "Who do you need to become to create the future you want?" It is a complex question and not easy to answer, but if you want to play bigger, you first have to shift your self-perception. (Remember how Amelia shifted her self-perception to become bold?)

This new leadership vision statement will encompass the future you want and enable people to shift their perception of you within the next three to six months.

Here is my leadership vision statement example from my time at Kraft for a little inspiration. (Note that I put the words I chose in bold—pun intended!)

Step 3: Reimagine—Where Do You Want to Go?

> *I am a **bold**, **visible** leader who has a reputation for **transforming** teams and organizations.*

Generating this statement changed everything for me. Remember who I was back then? Invisible. Told I was sitting in the back of the room in meetings, not participating, and not adding any value. Once I created this statement, I could no longer hide and hope to go unnoticed. Plus, I had to ensure that I focused on transforming my team and the organization wherever possible. I needed to be visible, so I sat at the executive table and spoke up, a bold move for me at the time.

Creating a powerful statement helps you to shift your mindset about yourself. Once you do, your actions and behaviors will follow.

Here are the current and new leadership vision statements from my client Sarah. There is nothing wrong with the original sentence; it captures who she is today. If she wants to play bigger, though, she needs to shift the language she uses and the beliefs she has about herself. I hope her example inspires you to imagine new possibilities for yourself too!

SARAH'S CURRENT LEADERSHIP VIEW STATEMENT:

I am an empathetic, kind leader who uses creativity and relationships to solve problems of all sizes for the organization.

SARAH'S NEW LEADERSHIP VISION STATEMENT:

I am a bold, decisive leader who confidently makes a visible impact on the business.

From the old statement to the new, Sarah's language gets stronger and more action oriented. The new statement will help her to step into her role with confidence, take different actions, and stay focused on what she needs to do so she doesn't fall back into old habits.

YOUR LEADERSHIP VISION EXERCISE

Now it is your turn to take your current leadership view statement and make it more powerful. How do you want to view yourself as a leader in the future? Shift your beliefs about yourself and you can show a different side to others. Without this mindset shift, you will sabotage anything new because you don't believe you are ready yet.

Remember my leadership vision statement from earlier? I had to use the new one to get motivated and push myself out of my comfort zone so I could sit at the table, speak up, and focus on transformation to show up differently. If you don't view yourself in a bigger way, no one else will either.

- In this exercise, you will create a leadership vision statement to help you become the person you aspire to be.
- Here are some places to look if you need ideas:
    - Review your answers to the exercises in Chapter 2. Are there any characteristics you want to shift or strengthen for the future?
    - Who are the people who inspire you in your company or community? What characteristics do they have that you wish you had too?
    - Have you observed something admirable in someone and said to yourself, *If only I could do what they can* or *How come I can't be more like so-and-so?* Those thoughts are your sign to rate yourself on those skills and qualities and decide if you want to strengthen them.

- Make sure the statement is big enough. Does reading it out loud make you feel uncomfortable, yet excited? If you answer yes, then you know it is perfect!

Create Your New Leadership Vision Statement

You can use the same template from earlier:

I am a(n) _____, _____ (2 adjectives) leader who _____ (verb) _____ (strength), and _____ (strength) to _____ (verb) _____ (outcome).

Or consider this shorter version:

I am a(n) _____, _____ (2 adjectives) leader who _____ (strength), to _____ (verb) _____ (outcome).

Write your new leadership vision statement here:

_____

_____

_____

Put this on a Post-it note that you can see every day.

You will need to revisit your leadership vision statement about every six months. The shift in you will happen faster than you expect, and you will need to stretch yourself again! Changing roles, especially if it is a promotion, is also a good opportunity to revisit your statement. You want to make sure you show up in a bigger way for the new role.

I would love to hear your leadership vision statement! Join my Facebook group and share your original and new statements with me![5]

- - - - - - - - - - - - - - - - - - -

FUTURE STATE VISION EXERCISE

You have been in the land of possibilities during this entire chapter! The reflection has pushed you out of your comfort zone and given you the opportunity to find more clarity on what you truly want. You have identified where you are today and created a new leadership vision. How can you make a bigger, more visible impact and influence others? Describe the future you want.

Step 3: Reimagine—Where Do You Want to Go?

Key Takeaways

What are the key takeaways from this chapter? What are you excited about? What did you learn from Step 3, where you reimagined your future and answered, "Where do you want to go?" that will help you achieve greater visibility?

Part 1: Visibility and Career Growth Framework

PART 2

FOUNDATIONS FOR SUCCESS

CORE | **PERSONAL BRANDING** | **SHOWING VALUE & BUILDING CONFIDENCE**

The Foundations for Success contain the knowledge and insights you need to help support you before you assess yourself further and take action in Part 3 of the workbook. Think of Part 2 as a short rest, a break to prepare you for the rest of your journey to greater visibility!

Chapter 4
CORE FOUNDATIONS

THE FOUR CORE FOUNDATIONS FROM *The Visibility Factor* are necessary for you to understand prior to continuing on to the next chapters. In this chapter, I explain these concepts, including what it means to be visible, and help you avoid pitfalls on your journey to self-discovery. If you have read *The Visibility Factor*, I ask you to read this chapter as a review and because I've included additional details in this workbook.

The exercises I've included here are the same ones I do in my workshops and in sessions with my clients. If you skip them, you will miss out on learning about yourself and understanding what holds you back from greater visibility. A client in a group that I lead called one of these upcoming exercises "one of the best we have done" due to the number of insights she gained by completing it. Trust me, this is a proven process.

Core Foundation 1 – What Is Visibility?

The core message of *The Visibility Factor* is, while hard work is important, to have career success, you need to be visible to your management so that they recognize your capabilities and consider you for new opportunities. Visibility isn't always top of mind, and people tend to operate on autopilot when they speak to their co-workers. Sharing whatever comes to mind is okay, but it won't move the needle in terms of how you are perceived. Intentionally planning what you share with people about yourself, your team, and your work is the secret sauce that will help you stand out. Every interaction is an opportunity to show the value you bring, so take advantage of any situation you can. I am getting a little passionate about visibility here. Blame it on my day job! I want you to get excited about the possibilities that visibility can bring you.

Let's step back for a minute, though, and start with a dictionary definition of visibility to ground you: *Merriam-Webster* defines visibility as "the quality or state of being visible."[6] Have you considered how *you* define visibility?

DEFINITION OF VISIBILITY EXERCISE

What is your definition of visibility and why do you define it that way?

....

....

....

....

....

....

....

About five months after I published the book, I started *The Visibility Factor* podcast. One of the four questions I ask all of my guests is how they define visibility. Here are some of their responses:

- Feeling seen and appreciated in ways that matter.
- Allowing yourself to be seen and heard.

- Showing up as joyous, calm, easy, and happy as I can, and aligned with my authentic self.
- The opportunity to shine your gifts and help others shine theirs so the world is a better place.
- An act of service. We hide because we're afraid, but when we hide, we deprive other people of the opportunity to take advantage of what we uniquely offer.
- Visibility is self-acceptance.
- Being seen for who you truly are.
- Visibility is the courage to know, show, and bestow yourself.
- Visibility is being a prominent, active presence with other people.

CREATE YOUR VISIBILITY DEFINITION EXERCISE

Now that you have seen more examples, do you want to change your original definition? Use any of the visibility definition examples if they resonate for you. If you changed your definition, why?

You might ask what my definition of visibility is:

> **BEING SEEN FOR WHO YOU TRULY ARE AS A LEADER AND THE VALUE THAT YOU BRING.**

If you don't put yourself out there and show your leadership that you are ready for the next step, they won't consider you for future opportunities.

When I lead workshops, one of my favorite places to start with the group is to ask them a few questions to gauge where they are in terms of their own visibility in that moment. Let's see how you respond to these questions.

OBSTACLES TO VISIBILITY EXERCISE

What prevents you from being more visible?

....

....

....

....

....

....

....

WHAT IS POSSIBLE? EXERCISE

What would be possible for you in your career if you were more visible?

....

....

....

....

....

....

....

....

....

....

....

The reason I ask these two questions is to show people that they are not alone; many others have the same challenges with visibility. Any guesses as to what the top answers are? Hint: You will find the answers in Core Foundation 2!

The PIE Model

Have you ever had a problem to solve, and the answer appeared in an article, on a podcast, or in a conversation just when you were about to give up?

When I was struggling with my own visibility, the Kraft IT group was invited to attend a lunch-and-learn session with Harvey J. Coleman, who wrote *Empowering Yourself: The Organizational Game Revealed*.[7] He talked about his book and the model that he uses to teach people what is most important when it comes to career success. Coleman's foundational message in the book is that your career success is based on your performance, image, and exposure (PIE).

Here are my summations of PIE:

- **Performance** – The day-to-day work you are responsible for and need to deliver.
- **Image** – How people see or perceive you; also known as your personal brand.
- **Exposure** – Who knows about you and what you do; taking opportunities to be in front of career influencers and decision-makers.

Coleman asked us to fill in the blanks of a circle graph and assign percentages for how much of our time was spent in each of the three areas he had identified. I saw his pie graph on the screen and immediately came up with my answers. I spent most of my time working hard to get everything done, so I put 70 percent on performance, 20 percent on image, and 10 percent on exposure.

How would you assign percentages to your own professional time?

WHERE DO YOU SPEND YOUR TIME? EXERCISE:

By percentage, how do you currently spend your time in these three areas?

PERFORMANCE _____ % IMAGE _____ % EXPOSURE _____ % = 100%

Imagine my surprise when he showed this pie chart illustrating the results of his research:

PIE Model*

Performance: The day-to-day work you are responsible for and need to deliver.

Image: How people see or perceive you; also known as your personal brand.

Exposure: Who knows about you and what you do? Taking opportunities to be in front of career influencers and decision-makers.

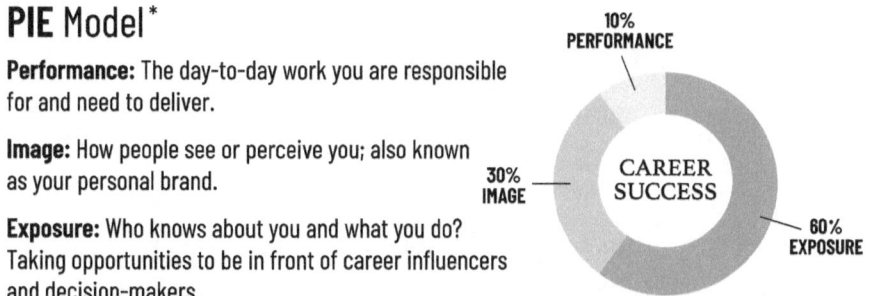

To have success in your career, you must focus on your brand and getting exposure while doing your job.

*Based on *Empowering Yourself: The Organizational Game Revealed* by Harvey J. Coleman

Figure 4.1: PIE Model

Coleman shared the following: "Performance drives only 10 percent of success, image drives 30 percent and exposure drives 60 percent." To be successful in your career, you need to build your brand and get exposure while you perform your job. To get new opportunities, you need to show that you are ready for them. You demonstrate readiness through the management of your image and finding ways to gain exposure so others can see you.

Up until the moment when Coleman shared his insights, I believed performance would drive the highest levels of success for me. I was wrong. In reality, it is the complete opposite. Doing your job is expected; therefore, performance is only 10 percent. If you aren't doing the minimum, you won't be moving up any time soon. You need to show your value and impact so that decision-makers see you as a leader who makes a difference in the company and is ready for more.

HOW WILL YOU SPEND YOUR TIME? EXERCISE

Now that you have read about the PIE model, how will you shift from your current percentages and spend your time in these three areas going forward?

> PERFORMANCE _____ % IMAGE _____ % EXPOSURE _____ % = 100%

Without exposure, people may not notice that you are ready for the next step in your career. Being in front of your management and other influencers allows you to show them your talents. When you have an opportunity to be visible, take advantage of it. And keep in mind, visibility isn't a one-time event. Showing your value and talents to others needs to become an intentional, consistent part of who you are as a leader in order to be effective.

When I was doing research for *The Visibility Factor*, I found a study that reinforces the importance of visibility when it comes to promotions. Over several years, the Center for Creative Leadership did a study on the "Realities of Management Promotion" with three major companies. They found one determining factor in 73 percent of cases where promotions were given: The person who got the promotion was visible to the decision-maker.[8] It is time for you to get in front of your decision-makers and show them you are ready!

Core Foundation 2 – The Role of Fear

Since *The Visibility Factor* came out, I have witnessed in workshop discussions and in coaching how common it is to identify with fears and challenges and use them as reasons to stay stuck. For example, if you label yourself an introvert, you may use that as a reason not to speak up in meetings. You may believe that there is something wrong with you and can't conceive of a way to change it. Fear takes over, and without an alternative path to follow, you are stuck in limbo between where you are and where you want to be.

When the pain is too great, you will be open to change. Remember in the introduction when I received feedback from a mentor that I wasn't visible and didn't show my value? I was shocked to hear that feedback in the moment, but when I reflected on it, I knew it was accurate. I had become complacent. I believed I was a "top talent," visible enough that I didn't need to put myself out there any further. For fear of judgment and criticism, I had created a story that kept me invisible. Sweet Perfect Sue had an image to uphold, and it was safer to hide. I believed these fears and played small.

Once I got this feedback, I knew I had to take a new approach. I asked a business mentor to help me understand what to do next and implement changes. I also hired a coach, worked with other mentors, studied what others around me did to be visible, and took actions to build my confidence and gain momentum. I didn't become visible overnight, but I began to believe in myself for the first time in my career. I was empowered to take simple actions that would move me out of hiding so I could be more visible and yet remain authentic.

This simple formula below is a recipe for confidence. Confidence requires that you believe in yourself plus take visible actions. It may seem as if confidence needs to come first, before you act, but it is truly your thoughts that drive your actions to help you show up differently and ultimately become confident. When workshop participants think of what would be possible for them if they were visible, confidence is the number one answer.

> **BELIEF IN YOURSELF + VISIBLE ACTIONS = CONFIDENCE**

You become visible when you stand out from the crowd, when you say or do something that puts the spotlight on you. Does the spotlight seem too scary and uncomfortable to consider? If so, you may decide to stay in the background. Fear is the number one reason my clients and workshop participants give for why they aren't visible. Fear can overpower you, keep you hidden from others, and push you to stay behind the scenes—and you may not recognize the unconscious choice you have made to stay out of the limelight.

Believe me, I had the exact same fear. Anytime I put myself out there in front of people, it was uncomfortable for me. There were many times in my corporate role when I avoided big presentations, speaking up in meetings with senior leaders, attending networking events, and speaking at conferences. I lacked confidence, so I didn't believe I could be visible and show up the way my management wanted me to be. Remember how my brain created stories to keep me safe when I was stressed? Our brains are amazing, but they can't tell the difference between real danger and non-threatening situations that create anxiety and fear.

I operated with a lot of doubts for many years, which led me to play small most of the time. What if I said or did the wrong things? What if people judged me? What if I never got another chance to show them I could do more? My fear of failure was powerful. I would have to take risks to show up differently, but the work I needed to do internally to remove old beliefs and stories was the bigger battle for me.

Here are some of the beliefs we may have about ourselves when fear is in the driver's seat and tries to control everything. These are from my own experience and what my clients have shared with me. Do any of them apply to you?

- You work hard, but don't stand out and aren't included in promotion discussions. You are stuck and can't figure out what you need to do to move up.
- You do what you are asked to do but receive feedback that what you do isn't enough and you need to take additional steps to be noticed. You have a perception problem and no idea how to solve it.

- You are in a new role as a manager and aren't sure how to manage a team. (This is the toughest transition a leader can make.) Leading people and the idea of gaining visibility are both new to you.
- You receive a promotion but continue to do what you have always done. This transition requires you to show your leadership in a bigger way than before, but you aren't sure how to do that and/or choose to avoid it.
- You move to a new company but struggle to get established and build credibility.
- You get feedback from others who say you are doing great; you just need to work on a few things and you will be ready for the next level. This happens repeatedly but nothing changes. You give up hope of getting the promotion anytime soon.

Thoughts and Limiting Beliefs

We all carry around many beliefs, assumptions, stories, and experiences that function as the "truth" for us until we are told differently or change out the old files for new ones. Much like computers, our brains access these files all day long and use them in all of our work and interactions.

For the sake of simplicity, I will group the four types of files (beliefs, assumptions, stories, and experiences) together and use the acronym "BASE" when referring to them. The BASE files are the foundation for how we view the world, make decisions, form opinions, figure out how to do things, and decide how we feel about people.

> **BASE = BELIEFS, ASSUMPTIONS, STORIES AND EXPERIENCES**

One of my old beliefs was that only senior leaders could sit at the "big table" at meetings. I would say to myself: *I respect them, and they are higher on the chain of command. I don't belong there because I am not on the executive team, and I don't have an IT education.* I believed that story for such a long time. I chose to sit at the back of the room and not participate because I thought I wasn't smart enough or at the right level. This was the invisibility story I created to stay safe. Hiding behind those who chose to be out front kept me from opportunities. Self-limiting beliefs can hold you back from what you want to achieve in life.

LIMITING BELIEF EXERCISE

What limiting belief or invisibility story have you told yourself to stay safe and in the background?

....

....

....

....

....

....

....

Byron Katie is the author of multiple books that help people see their thoughts in new ways. She says, "A thought is harmless unless we believe it."[9] If we understand that our thoughts are just thoughts and don't assign them any significance, they can't hurt us.

If you let go of the self-defeating messages in your head and no longer believed them, what would you do instead? What if you chose to believe something different and took different actions?

Any of the challenges I listed earlier in this chapter will trigger your brain and tell it that you are under stress. Remember, it will send critical messages to create fear and stop any new action in order to protect you. Understanding this concept helped me calm down when I experienced fear and simply see my brain as a protector, not a saboteur.

You may experience limiting beliefs, but now you will recognize them in yourself and in team members who also struggle. Leaders who use a coaching approach of asking questions about these beliefs can uncover the hidden stories preventing team members from reaching their potential and help to redirect them. (See the appendix in *The Visibility Factor* for a list of questions to use.)

Be open, shift your view of yourself, and trust that you can take these actions. I can say with complete certainty that I would not be where I am today if I hadn't learned how to create opportunities to show my value. Don't prejudge opportunities; they could do great things for your career if you can make a difference with your involvement.

You will face unexpected challenges. I want you to be kind to yourself, recognize when you do well, and forgive yourself when you could do better. Focus on the positive and it will change your outlook. Self-acceptance and patience with yourself are crucial in these moments. It sounds simple, but they are so important to help you move past all the negativity, criticism, and judgment that are probably coming from you more than anyone else. You are amazing just the way you are. You are worth it! Call it out for yourself.

The Self-Critic

I nicknamed my inner critic "Victoria." (She has a high opinion of herself and a UK accent, in case you are curious.) I appreciate how Victoria has kept me safe over the years, but at times she has also kept me from doing more. For instance, when I attended a networking event in 2012 while working for Kraft, Victoria had a lot to say: *You know that introverts aren't good at this networking stuff and never will be. If you talk to people, you will feel insecure and say things that don't make sense. Why would you risk the judgment? Why don't you get out of here and head home instead? We can put on some sweats and read that new book you got the other day. Wouldn't that be so much more fun?*

Victoria's voice used to be the loudest one in my head. It drove my decisions and behavior. Along with my people-pleasing, rule-following belief system, listening to her allowed me to hide and let others shine instead.

Our inner critics can be mean. I have had clients name their own inner critics, especially since it helps to address them by name when they are getting too loud and you need to tell them to be quiet! Your inner critic can take over your thoughts if you let it. Pay attention and recognize when it happens to avoid the trap.

In the next set of exercises, you will explore what your self-critic says to you. The only way to manage these critical messages is to recognize that they aren't real and you don't have to believe them.

Are you aware that 77,000 thoughts go through your head each day? Yes, I said 77,000! Your thoughts will come and go and there is no need to hold onto them if they are not helping you. You get to make the choice to either keep them or cast them aside.

NAMING YOUR SELF-CRITIC EXERCISE

What would be a good name for your self-critic? (It can be your own little secret!)

SELF-CRITIC EXERCISE

What are some of the negative and critical messages that your inner critic (insert the name you chose for them) says to you?

....

....

....

....

....

....

....

MESSAGING TURNAROUND EXERCISE

Take each of those messages and turn them into positive statements to help you shift away from limiting beliefs. (For example, if your current thought is *I can't get promoted*, you could articulate your new thought as something like *I deserve to be promoted and take new actions every day to show that I am ready.*)

....

....

....

....

Bragging vs. Visibility

The fear of being viewed as a braggart will hold you back from speaking up or sharing an opinion. I had the same concern at Kraft, where I had only witnessed people talk up their work in order to brag and engage in an off-putting level of self-promotion. Is there someone in your company who brags too much about their accomplishments in meetings? I have met plenty of people who have no idea they do it. It can become a hard habit for them to turn off. I assumed that the people who bragged were trying to get ahead without doing any work and only focused on the negative side of their behavior because to me, bragging and visibility were synonymous.

The differences between bragging and authentic visibility can be distinguished by the intention, tone, and content of the communication. Here are some examples that highlight the differences:

Core Foundations

BRAGGING	SITUATION	AUTHENTIC VISIBILITY
"I single-handedly completed this project ahead of schedule. It's obvious that I'm the most talented and efficient person on the team."	**PROJECT ACCOMPLISH-MENT**	"I'm proud to have contributed to the successful completion of this project. It was a team effort, and I'm grateful for the collaboration with and support of my colleagues."
"I'm the best coder in this company. Nobody can match my programming skills. I'm miles ahead of my colleagues."	**PROFESSIONAL SKILLS**	"I've been fortunate to develop my coding skills and am grateful for the opportunities to learn and grow. I'm excited to continue to build on my abilities and collaborate with other talented professionals."
"I just got promoted and received a substantial raise. I'm clearly more valuable to this company than anyone else here."	**PROMOTION OR RAISE**	"I'm thrilled to share that I've been promoted and received a raise. I'm grateful for the opportunities for growth and the trust placed in me. I'm looking forward to doing more to contribute to the company's success."
"I won the Employee of the Year award! It's obvious that I'm the most exceptional and indispensable person in this organization."	**RECOGNITION OR AWARD**	"I'm honored to have received the Employee of the Year award. This recognition motivates me to continue to work hard and support my colleagues in achieving their goals."
"My team is the best in the company. We always outperform everyone else, and no one can match our skills and achievements. We are simply unbeatable."	**LEADER TALKING ABOUT A TEAM**	"I'm incredibly proud of my team's accomplishments. Their hard work, dedication, and innovative thinking have consistently resulted in outstanding outcomes. I believe in the talent and collaboration within our team."

Figure 4.2: Bragging vs. Visibility

Can you identify the differences between bragging and authentic visibility now? You will work on your own examples and learn ways to reframe them in later chapters.

Self-Sabotage

I know what to do—why don't I do it?

The leader of the meeting had asked for volunteers to go first, but I couldn't figure out how to step up to the front of the room to present. It was an invisible barrier comprised of my own fear, and I couldn't break through it; I would only do it if someone forced me to. What the hell was I so scared of?

Once I learned what actions to take to become more visible, I assumed it would be easy; but fear took over and I was unprepared. It is important to be aware of this challenge in case you find yourself in a similar place where you can't seem to move forward.

I used to hide behind strong leaders and let them share their ideas instead of speaking up to share my own. I couldn't see my own value. I dismissed and rationalized to avoid taking any actions that might change the opinion I had of myself. I wanted to stay in the background and under the radar.

Brad Yates, speaker, author, and coach, describes self-sabotage as "misguided self-love. That fear and resistance—generally based on old misunderstandings (yours or someone else's)—stops you from being, doing and having what you want."[10]

If we recognize self-sabotage as a simple misunderstanding based on our mind trying to keep us safe at that moment, we can replace our lens and reframe what is happening. It is clear to me now that I once used self-sabotage as a protective mechanism to take myself out of the game before I could fail or be hurt. The beliefs were my reality at the time, and they created blind spots. Has this happened to you? What do your beliefs tell you about yourself? If your thoughts and beliefs don't support you, they could cause you to take a detour from the journey you want to be on and the goals you want to achieve.

SABOTAGE EXERCISE

When do you find yourself in sabotage mode as a form of self-protection?

....

....

....

....

Here is a deeper explanation of what happens when resistance shows up for you. Your stress increases when you try something new and sets off the alert mode in your brain. Your nervous system can't tell the difference between something that is new and something that is putting you in danger, so to keep you safe, your brain does the only thing it knows how to do and sends out a warning message like "You aren't good enough" or "You shouldn't apply for that role." This voice is rightly called an inner critic because it sends out critical messages to push you to resist and stop you from acting. It plants doubts in your mind about your skills and if you let it take over, it will kill your confidence.

RESISTANCE EXERCISE

When do you experience resistance to taking action?

....

....

....

....

The good news is, you don't have to listen to the criticism now that you understand the underlying motivation. Thank your brain for keeping you safe, but don't stop there. Continue to move out of your comfort zone and lean into being uncomfortable so you can take new actions, gain confidence, and show that you are ready for the next move in your career. People will recognize that you are playing bigger.

It takes time to rewire those old habits, but remember, you are not alone. I will be with you, supporting you every step of the way.

· · · · · · · · · · · · · · · · · · ·

BE PREPARED EXERCISE

It's good to be prepared. What do you plan to do when you self-sabotage or resist moving forward?

....

....

....

....

....

....

....

....

....

....

....

Core Foundation 3 – Programming (aka Stories)

I was the firstborn, and I wanted my parents to be proud of me. The truth is, I wanted to please my family and have their approval. I continued to strive for perfection with my teachers and, as an adult, with my managers. Does this sound familiar? I grew accustomed to external validation, and without it, I internalized the message that I had failed in some way. Without the pat on the back, I had no barometer to tell me how I was performing. I hadn't learned how to trust myself and find validation within.

Many of the old stories and programming that lived in my head came from what I learned as a child and internalized into adulthood. You would assume that new stories replace childhood ones as you get older, but they don't until you become aware of the old tapes.

In 2015, KPMG International published a study on women's leadership. The research participants included 3,000 women aged eighteen to sixty-four. One of the main questions the participants were asked was, "What are the lessons that you learned growing up?" The results of the study showed that women internalized messages they heard as children and that those messages continued to influence their behavior as adults.

Here are a few of the responses to the question, from highest to lowest percentages:

- 86 percent: Be nice to others.
- 86 percent: Be a good student.
- 85 percent: Be respectful to authorities.
- 77 percent: Be helpful.
- 56 percent: Take a stand for what you believe in.
- 44 percent: Be a good leader.
- 34 percent: Share your point of view.[11]

All of us were indoctrinated as children in one way or another. When I came into the world, it was expected that I would be a perfect good girl who stayed quietly in the background. Husbands worked outside the home and made the money; women stayed home and raised the kids. What is valued in women and girls, boys and men has shifted over the years, but for many generations, this was what we were taught.

RULES EXERCISE:

Do you have "rules" that you learned when you were young and still believe you need to follow?

....

....

....

....

....

....

....

....

....

....

....

....

....

....

Core Foundation 4 – Six Types of Impostor Syndrome

Impostor syndrome is the term for when you don't believe that you are good enough, smart enough, or ready for something bigger. The irony of the term is that this syndrome impacts the people who are high achievers, not actual impostors. High achievers accomplish so much but still don't believe they are successful.

The messages that once played on constant repeat in my head were *I'm not good enough* and *Someone is going to tell me I am a fraud because I am not smart enough to be in this new role*. To keep you safe, impostor syndrome keeps you out of the action.

Lack of self-trust and comparison to others reinforce the cycle of self-doubt. Self-doubt shows up for everyone at one time or another, but most often when there is something new to do. Resistance to acting and fear of failure will prevent any forward motion toward a goal.

Impostor syndrome impacts everyone at one time or another. Even famous people experience it. Maya Angelou, who passed away in 2014 and was a poet, singer, film director, civil rights activist, Grammy winner, and Presidential Freedom Award winner, said, "I have written eleven books, but each time I think, uh oh, they're going to find out now. I've run a game on everybody, and they're going to find me out."[12] Tom Hanks, an Oscar-winning actor who has made over seventy films and TV shows, is quoted as saying, "No matter what we've done, there comes a point where you think, 'How did I get here? When are they going to discover that I am, in fact, a fraud and take everything away from me?'"[13]

Research began in 1978 on impostor syndrome and has continued to evolve over the years. Initially only believed to impact women, it has now been shown that it affects both women and men, but in different and diverse ways.

Overachievers with impostor syndrome have strong values and want to master things. Impostor syndrome rises to the surface when you want to be good at something and avoid failure. *If I can't do it well, maybe I shouldn't try. If I don't draft the article or make the speech, no one will see me; therefore, I won't fail.* Such self-critical thoughts and comparisons to others can make you believe that you don't belong and aren't good enough. And if you judge and criticize yourself first, no one else needs to do it. You remain perfect in their eyes.

I feel like a phony.
I don't deserve my success.
I'm not who they think I am.

Have you ever said these phrases to yourself? If so, you might have a case of impostor syndrome. And you aren't alone; studies have found that 70 percent of all people feel like impostors at one time or another.[14] Still, if you are impacted by impostor syndrome, there are easy actions you can take to help you move through it.

Types and Traits of Impostor Syndrome

Here is a summary of the six types of impostor syndrome, the common behaviors and ideas associated with them, and actions that will help you manage your specific type. Check out the summary and then complete the following exercise.

PEOPLE-PLEASING AND LACK OF BOUNDARIES

Behaviors to Look for with These Types	What to Do Differently
<ul><li>Focused on making others happy</li><li>Want to be liked</li><li>Regard others' needs as more important than their own</li><li>Do not say no to any requests</li><li>Involved in one-sided relationships</li><li>Frequently taken advantage of</li></ul>	**People Pleasing**<ul><li>Value your own work and communicate your priorities when people ask for your help</li><li>Determine the urgency of the request</li><li>Don't automatically say yes!</li></ul>**Lack of Boundaries**<ul><li>Have prepared responses to help you say no</li><li>Assess whether the people around you are taking your energy</li><li>View boundaries as good for you, not bad</li></ul>

COMPARISON AND PLAYING SMALL

Behaviors to Look for with These Types	What to Do Differently
<ul><li>Seek external validation</li><li>Focused on others' plans and ideas</li><li>Defer to others when making decisions</li><li>Assume that everyone else knows more than they do</li></ul>	**Comparison**<ul><li>Be proud of your own success</li><li>Remind yourself that everyone has their own strengths and gifts</li><li>Compare yourself only with yourself (not others)</li></ul>**Plays Small**<ul><li>Find people who believe in you to support you</li><li>Believe what people tell you about what you are good at</li><li>Don't take things personally</li></ul>

PROCRASTINATION AND PERFECTION

Behaviors to Look for with These Types	What to Do Differently
<ul><li>Put things off and don't start them</li><li>Overanalyze things and hesitate to make decisions</li><li>Afraid to fail, so don't try</li><li>Afraid to start things because of fear that it won't be good enough</li><li>Struggle to make decisions for fear of being wrong</li></ul>	**Procrastination**<ul><li>Take imperfect action to get started</li><li>Ask yourself what you are avoiding that needs to move forward</li><li>Ask yourself what is distracting you from doing what you should be doing</li></ul>**Perfection**<ul><li>Be mindful of the expectations that you have of yourself and others</li><li>Follow the 80/20 rule: Is 80% good enough to move forward vs. spending 20% more time that won't make a difference?</li></ul>

Figure 4.3: People Pleasing and Lack of Boundaries

IMPOSTOR SYNDROME TYPES EXERCISE

What impostor syndrome type do you resonate with most? How does it challenge and impact you?

....

....

....

....

....

....

....

....

....

....

....

....

....

....

....

....

....

....

Reflection

You did it! You made it to the last exercise of this chapter. You have done the work to solidify your understanding of the big foundational concepts from the book. This important step has grounded you in an understanding of visibility and what could get in the way of your success.

This last exercise helps you reflect on specific scenarios.

VISIBILITY TIMELINE EXERCISE:

In this exercise, you will build a "visibility timeline" to help you identify times when—and patterns where—visibility helped you or the lack of visibility hurt you. The purpose of the timeline is to review what has taken place in your career and life from a visibility perspective. This is one of the highest-rated exercises that I do with people, and it can shift how you view your past experiences. You will leverage the timeline results in upcoming exercises.

Here is an example from a client of mine who went through the timeline exercise.

NANCY'S STORY

Nancy was studying her completed visibility timeline and remarked, "I just had an aha moment." "What was it?" I asked. She shared, "I included a situation when I was told I didn't have enough experience to interview for a role I wanted. Until I did this exercise, I had no idea that I had internalized the message of not having enough experience, and that belief kept me from interviewing for any other roles for five more years.

FIVE MORE YEARS! Years later, I found out that it wasn't that I didn't have enough experience, it was that the hiring manager didn't know me and wouldn't take a chance on someone he hadn't seen in action."

Nancy believed the "you don't have enough experience" story that HR told her during that interview process. She had to find a way to rationalize what had happened, so she told herself she was happy in her current role and uninterested in change. This kept her safe from rejection but also limited her ability to move up. The fear of rejection is powerful. After completing the visibility timeline exercise, Nancy recognized how that story had impacted her, causing her to play small and miss out on opportunities.

Now it is your turn. On the next page, you will see a chart that is divided into two columns. Here are the steps:

1. In the boxes below "Visibility Opportunities Missed," note up to three situations—in detail and with dates—in which you held yourself back from visibility. Include how each of those decisions impacted you.
2. In the boxes below "Visibility Opportunities Taken," note up to three situations when you were visible—also in detail and with dates—and discuss how each of those decisions affected you.

VISIBILITY TIMELINE

Visibility Opportunities Missed	Visibility Opportunities Taken
Date:	**Date:**
Date:	**Date:**
Date:	**Date:**

What do you notice when you look at the events on your timeline? Do you see any new insights? What is clear to you now that you couldn't see back then?

Is there a pivotal moment on your timeline that led you to an unexpected path of visibility?

....

....

....

....

....

....

....

Can you now recognize a pattern in when or where you chose visibility vs. not being visible?

....

....

....

....

....

....

....

What stands out to you from your descriptions of the situations in the "Visibility Opportunities Taken" column on your timeline? What helped you to become visible? (For example, were you bolder or more confident, or was there something else that helped you in that situation?)

....
....
....
....
....
....
....
....

Are you still leveraging any of those same qualities or strengths today?

....
....
....
....
....
....
....
....

Did you notice anything that you used to do but haven't tried in a while or that you forgot about and could use to help you stand out now?

....

....

....

....

....

....

....

Key Takeaways

Did you experience any new aha moments as you read this chapter? What did you learn by going through the exercises? Take notes below so you have them to refer to and use for later exercises.

....

....

....

....

....

....

....

Part 2: Foundations for Success

PS: If you find this workbook helpful, I would love it if you would leave a review wherever you purchased it. I learned after publishing my first book that reviews are very helpful in getting your book in front of more people so you can help *them*! If you haven't left an online review before, you can simply share your favorite parts and how this workbook helped you. Thank you in advance!

Chapter 5
PERSONAL BRANDING FOUNDATION

Inside Chapter 5

In this chapter, you will learn why managing your personal brand (a.k.a. your image), and the way people perceive you, is so important. In a *Harvard Business Review* article titled, "Creating a Positive Professional Image," Mallory Stark interviewed Harvard Business School professor Laura Morgan Roberts, whose research focuses on professional image.

"As HBS professor Laura Morgan Roberts sees it, if you aren't managing your own professional image, others are. 'People are constantly observing your behavior and forming theories about your competence, character, and commitment, which are rapidly disseminated throughout your workplace.'"[15]

Everything you do either helps or hurts your brand. It is important to be aware of how you are perceived so you can adjust if needed. Remember, you want decision-makers to see the best of you, and this starts with what they already are aware of or have heard about you.

Your own understanding of your personal brand will help you when it comes to identifying action items to focus on in Part 3.

DAVE'S STORY

Dave was a mid-career leader who was struggling to get to the next level. When I met him for our first coaching session, he relayed some of his challenges. Organizational changes had impacted his group, and he had picked up the work from employees who had left the company and he had become overwhelmed. As we talked, other things came to light that could be affecting his boss's perception of him. He knew there were times when he wasn't aligned with his manager's priorities and that he wasn't meeting his due dates. He was hoping to figure out how to get back on track through coaching.

Managing Your Personal Brand and Others' Perceptions

Do you remember the PIE chart from Chapter 4? What was your answer when you were asked how much of your time was spent on your image? As a reminder, according to Harvey J. Coleman, 30 percent of your time needs to be spent on your image in order for you to achieve career success.[16] If your number was much lower than 30 percent, you can change it now.

DAVE'S PERSONAL BRAND

I asked Dave, "What do you think people would say if you asked them what your personal brand is?" He replied, "I have never asked anyone about my personal brand before, and I am not sure what it means. I only know some of the feedback I have received." "Okay," I said, "let's go through personal branding so you can better understand it and figure out what you want it to be."

Personal branding is the intentional, strategic practice of defining and expressing your value. "It's the amalgamation of the associations, beliefs, feelings, attitudes, and expectations that people collectively hold about you," according to *Harvard Business Review*.[17] Below is the same process that Dave and I went through to clarify and strengthen his personal brand.

PERSONAL BRAND AND PERCEPTION CHALLENGES

Here is a list of personal brand and perception challenges shared by my clients during coaching sessions. Check the boxes next to challenges that resonate for you.

- ☐ My personal brand is okay but needs to be stronger.
- ☐ I don't sell myself or my ideas well.
- ☐ I'm worried about my perception. I fear rejection and judgment from others.
- ☐ I want to project a stronger image in the organization.
- ☐ I have no idea how I am perceived.
- ☐ I have to wear a mask to conform to how others want me to be.
- ☐ I don't take the time to pay attention to my personal brand.
- ☐ I want to create a career vision and be empowered to play bigger.
- ☐ If I am more visible, people won't see me as relatable to them anymore.
- ☐ I don't advocate for myself and ask for what I want.
- ☐ I am unsure how to manage my career.
- ☐ I worry if my team isn't doing well. I need to save them, so it doesn't reflect on me.
- ☐ I am afraid that if I achieve too much success, I will get too much recognition and won't fit in with my friends and family anymore.
- ☐ I am not sure how to position myself for the job I want.
- ☐ I found out my personal brand isn't good, and I don't know how to improve it.

Part 2: Foundations for Success

I listed fifteen challenges here. How many apply to you? ....

Pick up to three challenges from the list that you want to focus on while you work on this chapter.

1. ....
   ....

2. ....
   ....

3. ....
   ....

If someone asked you what your personal brand is, what would you say? Let's explore some questions to help you learn about the different parts of a personal brand and take a look at your own, current personal brand.

• • • • • • • • • • • • • • • • • • • •

PERSONAL BRAND EXERCISE

Answer the following questions to start building your personal brand statement.

1. How would I describe myself in three to five words?
   ....

2. How do other people describe me? ....
   ....
   ....
   ....

3. What am I known for? (Strengths, values, interests, etc.)

　

4. What do I do better than anyone else?

　

5. What value can I offer to my community/industry/network/company?

　

6. What stands out from these answers that I want people to learn about me?

Is your brand what you want it to be? You can turn it around if it isn't. What you do and say creates a perception of you in others, and if you are making a shift to reinvent your brand, consistency and intention will help you get there.

> ""YOUR PROFESSIONAL IMAGE IS THE SET OF QUALITIES AND CHARACTERISTICS THAT REPRESENT PERCEPTIONS OF YOUR COMPETENCE AND CHARACTER AS JUDGED BY YOUR KEY CONSTITUENTS (I.E. CLIENTS, COLLEAGUES, SUPERIORS, SUBORDINATES, ETC.)."[18]

Here is an example of how Sara Blakely has described her personal brand:

"24 years ago today I quit my job selling fax machines to start @spanx. I was so nervous, had absolutely no experience in fashion and $5,000 set aside of my savings, AND my headquarters was my apartment but I had BIG DREAMS."[19]

And here is the information in her "About" section on LinkedIn:

"Mom of 4. Inventor of Spanx. Afraid to fly. Refuse to give up my scrunchie. Believe it's my calling to support women."[20]

PERSONAL BRAND STATEMENT EXERCISE

Your personal brand statement is basically a catchphrase that tells others about your expertise and what makes you unique. People reading the statement should quickly understand exactly what you can do and what you specialize in.

What can you tell about who Sara is now that you have seen her personal brand statement and her LinkedIn "About" section?

....

....

....

....

....

....

Try drafting your own personal brand statement based on the answers you came up with to the questions in the personal brand statement exercise.

....

....

....

....

....

....

We have reviewed the positive side of personal brand, but what happens when something is hurting it? Here are a few examples of real-life situations that can reflect negatively on your personal brand and how you are perceived.

WHY IT HAPPENS/ NEGATIVE EFFECTS	WHAT YOU SHOULD DO
Picking up work for other people who have left the company instead of pushing for a replacement.	
You want to support the company and pick up extra work (people-pleasing), but then you get overwhelmed and can't get your own work done.	Advocate for a plan and timeline to replace the individuals and discuss current work that will be temporarily delayed while supporting what is needed in the interim.
Stepping in to do the work for a problem employee to keep anyone from noticing.	
You are afraid to speak up or look bad as their manager (insecurity and fear) but know it will eventually come to light and people will question why you are doing nothing about the problem employee.	Have direct, documented conversations with the problem employee. If things don't change, go to HR and discuss a performance improvement plan. Leverage company competencies and performance management processes. Keep management in the loop.
Taking on more work from other teams and not pushing back.	
You want to help (people-pleasing/lack of boundaries) from an image perspective, but this means you and your team are overstretched.	Before agreeing to take on more work, have a conversation so you understand what the work is and its urgency compared to your other work. Then decide what you and your team will or won't be able to do.
Fixing mistakes instead of pushing back when incomplete work comes in from another group because it seems simpler.	
You are trying to be nice (not holding boundaries) and not make a big deal out of something. But how much time does this take away from your own work?	Send the work back and explain the issue. If necessary, bring the concern to the group's management to ask them to provide additional training for the group.
The team can't do anything on their own and when you are out, things fall apart.	
You feel like you have to know everything and make it perfect, which leads to you micromanaging the team and them feeling like you don't trust them and they can't do anything without your approval.	A team needs to own their work and be trusted and empowered to handle things without their leader giving them all the answers. Coach them when they make mistakes so they learn how to do things without you. Lead, grow, and develop them.
You keep answering your team's questions instead of coaching them to figure out the solutions on their own.	
It feels easier to simply answer questions (not holding boundaries), but it isn't teaching them how to problem-solve and research to come up with their own answers.	Focus on helping the team learn how to solve problems so they don't rely on you to be the answer person.

Figure 5.1: Negative Effects and What You Should Do

In each of these cases, the personal brand of the leader or individual is impacted in a negative way—and they may have no idea it is happening. They believe that they are helping or supporting, but they are focused on the wrong things based on the expectations for their current role. Every single one of these situations will sow doubt and call their leadership and capabilities into question.

Would you have considered these as strikes against someone's brand? Do you have any negative personal brand situations that you (or your team, if you have one) need to address?

Get Your Own Feedback

I am a big proponent of asking for feedback on how you are doing from your manager and other key stakeholders. Many people aren't proactive about this, though, due to fears of what they might hear. They assume the worst and prefer to wait for the annual performance review process, when most people get feedback. When I attended a session about feedback with a consultant, she said, "Feedback should never have a birthday"—meaning that only getting feedback annually is not enough! If you haven't gathered enough feedback on your personal brand and performance, here is a way to get some.

DAVE'S OPPORTUNITY TO GET FEEDBACK

Dave wasn't clear on whether his boss saw him as a leader or not. He had recently had his midyear performance review and discovered that his manager hadn't asked anyone else for feedback on him. I asked Dave if he would be willing to seek out more feedback on how he is perceived on his own. He was open to it but wondered how best to go about it. I walked Dave through the approach I use with many of my clients.

This is a list of questions I have put together over the years from various feedback opportunities. When you want to request feedback, you can pick from the list or use your own questions.

360-DEGREE FEEDBACK EXERCISE

This exercise is intended to help you gain a 360-degree view of yourself. We all have blind spots, and this exercise helps to uncover them for you.
Here are the steps:

1. Create a feedback survey using the below questions to learn more about who you are to other people.
2. Choose five of the questions you want to include in your survey that will help you learn more about yourself.
3. Select a survey approach. Use any type of survey form you want, or email to get the answers.
4. Send the survey to ten to fifteen people, like your manager, co-workers, friends, and family members.
5. Pull the results together in a spreadsheet and identify any trends or patterns.

Here is the list of questions to choose from:

- When you think of me, what five adjectives come to mind?
- What do you believe I do to stand out from my peers?
- If I were a breed of dog, what type would I be and why?
- If you were to come to me for advice, what you would ask me about?
- What could I do differently that would have the greatest impact on my success?
- What are my strengths as a leader?
- What do you most appreciate or respect about me?

- Is there anywhere that I may be overusing a strength? What effects does this have?
- What one thing do you most recommend I do differently to be a more effective leader? Why, and what impact could this change have?
- What words of encouragement or advice can you offer me?
- What should I start, stop, or continue doing?

These questions are fun and will generate interesting responses! Ask the respondents to be honest. (I tell clients who are a little apprehensive about the survey process to tell respondents that their coach asked them to do this. You have my permission to do the same!)

This survey process can induce some fear simply because you don't know what the results will be. Let me reassure you that every time a client has done it, they have been so excited to receive the responses. It is hard to view yourself through another person's eyes unless they tell you what they observe and admire about you.

What are some of the key trends and patterns you have identified based on the survey results? Are there any gaps you need to focus on to be ready for future roles?

....

....

....

....

....

....

....

You could send a note to your respondents to say thanks for the feedback. Visibility bonus points, though, if you thank them *and* build a relationship with them. Set up a time to discuss what they shared with you and what actions you will take because of their feedback.

Performance Reviews

In many organizations, the only time detailed feedback is given is during an annual performance review, which isn't often enough. That is why I have my clients leverage the 360-degree feedback exercise so they can gather their own feedback throughout the year and take action sooner.

People in organizations understand why performance reviews are necessary, but instead of seeing them as great opportunities to tout your accomplishments and talk about your development, you might see them as another item on your to-do list.

Team members resist writing the self-assessment portion of their review for other reasons, though. It is easier to stay busy doing things than it is to slow down to focus on themselves. In my experience, it is a vulnerable process to rate yourself, write about the results of your work, and share what you want to do next. You might wonder, *What if my manager disagrees with my self-assessment?* (You will see a story about this type of situation in Chapter 10.) You may believe that writing a review doesn't do anything for you, but it lasts longer than this one role and current manager. Your manager's manager, human resources, and future managers will read it as well. You should take advantage of the opportunity to put your best into it.

You can take the simple approach and only include the basics of what you did during the year, but then you (probably unknowingly and unintentionally) send the message that you don't care about your career. Do you truly believe you have done good work this year? This is a visibility opportunity to include the impact and value those accomplishments had on the business in your review. What if your manager has no idea what you did because you didn't share it with them? It is your responsibility to ensure that you tell them. Write strategically about your accomplishments and what you want in your career.

Here are before and after examples of a review response:

Simple Review Response:
Delivered ABC project on time and on budget.

Value and Impact Review Response:
Delivered ABC project on time and on budget. Navigated resource constraints and accommodated late scope changes that the business identified were missing in earlier review sessions. The team delivered under an aggressive timeline. The clients provided great feedback about the project and nominated the team for an award.

It isn't enough to simply say what you did; you have to talk about it from a **value** and **impact** perspective. What feedback would you get from your manager if you took the second approach instead of the first for all your results? What if you did this throughout the year, not just in your performance review?

You have the ability to create the narrative about you through everything you do. This is one example of many, so don't miss out on opportunities. I had so many team members just do the simple version and send them to me. I sent them right back and said, "This is your opportunity to talk about your results. Take advantage of it."

Playing to Win vs. Playing Not to Lose

The concept of "playing to win vs. playing not to lose" was first discussed in *Playing to Win*, often referred to as a playbook for companies to win against the competition. The authors emphasize that a true strategy is about making bold choices aimed at winning, not merely avoiding failure or maintaining the status quo. In their words, "a too-modest aspiration is far more dangerous than a too-lofty one." This concept has been adopted by many as a way to describe the mindset and performance of people specifically in the contexts of business and sports.[21]

> ## DAVE'S PERCEPTION OF HIS PERFORMANCE
>
> "I can't do that."
>
> During a coaching session, Dave said this in response to feedback from his survey results: A few people had suggested that he could take more initiative, influence more decisions for his projects, and get more visibility by speaking at conferences about the innovative work he has done. I asked, "Why do you think you can't do that?" His response was telling. He said, "Who would want to hear from me? The people who speak at conferences are experts and I don't see myself as an expert at all." I paused for a moment; I understood what he was going through. I had been in his shoes years ago when I too was asked to speak at a conference. Finally, I said, "You have a goal to be more visible. Has it changed?" He shook his head no. I said, "You always get to choose what you want. You can 'play to win' by speaking at a conference or you can 'play not to lose' and continue to stay in the background. People who play to win take risks and do things that are out of their comfort zone. This is how you grow and show that you are ready for more. It seems as if the people who responded to the survey want to see more from you." He smiled and said, "That's true. I have been playing not to lose for a long time, and it isn't working. It's time for me to play to win now!"

The next table describes the characteristics of someone who plays to win vs. someone who plays not to lose. Assess yourself and your actions against this list. Are you playing to win or playing not to lose most of the time?

PLAYING TO WIN	PLAYING NOT TO LOSE
Confident	Has low or no self-confidence
Secure	Insecure
Takes risks	Risk-averse
Stands out	Blends in
Is proactive	Reactive
Leads	Follows
Challenges	Goes along with the crowd
Values themselves	Undervalues themselves

Figure 5.2: Playing to Win or Playing Not to Lose

If you find yourself in a situation where you are playing not to lose, you have a choice. What can you do to get back on track?

When you don't have confidence or feel secure, you play not to lose. You play it safe and avoid risks at all costs. When you are low on confidence, you need to try things that move you out of your comfort zone. *Actions* are what will restore or grow your confidence.

HOW DO YOU SHOW UP? EXERCISE

Are you playing to win or playing not to lose?

....

....

How would others assess you in this regard?

....

....

....

....

....

....

Career Planning

We started this journey by reflecting on and gauging where you have been, where you are now, and where you want to go next. You have answered so many of the key questions about your career; with your newfound clarity, it is now time to start sharing your vision for your career with others.

> **DAVE'S CAREER PLANNING**
>
> Although Dave was happy in his current role, he mentioned on more than one occasion that he had ambitions to move up to the next level. I asked him how clear he was on what a possible next step might be. He shared, "I can see myself moving into my manager's role in the next few years." I asked, "What do you need to work on to be ready for a managerial role?" He assessed what he believed he needed and where he currently stood.

Conversations about next career steps are good for any leader to have with their team members, and for team members to bring up with their managers. To be sure the conversation is productive and worthwhile, team members should be clear about what they are interested in doing. Spend some time back in Chapter 3 using the Career Clarity Framework if you need some support. Your manager and other influencers can only help you when they know what you want to do.

If asked, what will you say you want to do? It doesn't have to be a specific role, but you do need to be clear enough to give your manager a starting point: "I want to lead the supply chain logistics organization for North America." If you're not clear on exactly what position yet, you can say something like, "I want to lead a large team working on high growth and transformational programs, in a role that offers me the opportunity to define strategy, influence the future, and have decision-making authority." Both examples allow for a conversation to take place about these roles, whether or not your manager perceives that you are ready for them, and if not, what you need to do to be ready.

FUTURE CAREER CONVERSATION EXERCISE

Share where you want to go next in your career with no constraints or limitations—just list some ideas to consider. This is a good exercise to do when you have plenty of time to work on it.

....

....

....

....

Part 2: Foundations for Success

Add some talking points here, what you would communicate to others about your next steps and what excites you about them. (Hint: If you aren't excited, why would anyone else be?)

Your Personal Brand Bank Account

You may already have heard about the concept of a personal brand bank account, but I want you to understand how to leverage it and why it is important to manage.

If the concept is new to you, it is similar to your financial bank accounts, only the balance is determined by what you have done to strengthen or weaken your personal brand. Everything you do well adds deposits into your bank account, and your balance will continue to compound over the years of service you give to the company and/or industry. If you ever have an issue, you can use the goodwill you have built up in your bank account to help you out of a difficult situation. Keep adding good things to your account and maintain your positive reputation.

It is also similar to a real bank account in that, if there is no money in the account, you have nothing to spend. You may have used it all, or you may be new to the company and just getting started. It will take time for you to build up the account from where it is now to the point where you can leverage it when you need it.

PERSONAL BRAND BANK ACCOUNT EXERCISE

How would you characterize your personal brand bank account? (Is it overflowing, is it just okay, or does it need some help?)

....

....

....

....

....

....

....

....

What can you do to keep increasing the balance in the account?

....

....

....

....

Key Takeaways

Your personal brand and how you are perceived need to be top of mind. When your brand and general perception are positive, it can help you move to a new role. Keep doing things to increase the balance in your personal brand bank account.

What did you learn about your personal brand and the way you are perceived? Do you need to make any changes?

Part 2: Foundations for Success

Chapter 6
SHOWING VALUE AND BUILDING CONFIDENCE FOUNDATION

Inside Chapter 6

In this chapter, we will:

- Take a closer look at what might be holding you back;
- Give you a glimpse into how to focus on value first;
- Help you recognize the importance of being an equal with others;
- Dive deeper into self-worth, identity, and self-trust; and
- Learn why you need to be your own advocate.

I've included stories, examples, and exercises to help you learn what actions you can take to grow in value and confidence in both your career and your personal life. Follow my client Lori's journey along the showing value and building confidence path to open up awareness of the places where you may be holding back your value and dimming your confidence. Focusing on those things will be powerful for you.

Pay attention to opportunities to work on things here that you can later act on in Part 3. If you need to pause along the way, that is absolutely okay. This is important work, so do what you need to do here. Just keep going, no matter what!

LORI'S STORY

"I don't belong in the room with my group."

Lori said this to me after I asked why she felt hesitant about her new role. When I met her, she had recently accepted this new job and moved across the country to take it. She was excited when she talked about it and her potential to make a difference there. So why did she believe she didn't belong? What finally came to light was that she was working for a group of lawyers, and she had put them on a pedestal. Though she was extremely accomplished, Lori had no idea what she could possibly offer that would be of value to them.

Discovering Your BASE Files

Your brain has latched onto old stories (*I'm not good enough, I'm not smart enough, others are better at this than I am, I tried this before and it didn't work*) that hold you back. When you try something new, your brain says, *Wait a minute, you are doing something new and I'm not sure you should be doing it.* Believing the message prevents you from acting. As a result, you doubt yourself and your confidence takes a hit. Remember when I talked about BASE files in Chapter 4?

DISCOVERING LORI'S BASE FILES

Lori did not have a law degree; therefore, in her mind, she didn't belong in the room. I understood what she was going through. I had been the person who told herself she didn't belong at the table with the executives because she didn't have an IT degree. Remember learning about impostor syndrome in Chapter 4? This is a prime example of comparing yourself to others and feeling self-doubt when you see a gap between you and them.

Your brain accesses the four types of BASE files much like a computer retrieves files. (You may be saying to yourself, *Another IT example, Sue?* Bear with me, this is the easiest way to explain how this works!) When you need to retrieve a file on your computer, the system finds it and shows you the most recent files based on your search criteria. Your brain operates in the same way, bringing up the most recent files that align with what you need. The challenge is that the file you pull up might be good—or it might be out of date and corrupt.

Here's a quick example to show you how bad files can impact relationships and communication. You see Tom from across the cafeteria and your brain finds the most recent BASE file on him from five years ago to help you remember him. The file reminds you that Tom was difficult to work with and cut you off in meetings all the time. Because it is your most recent file, you expect him to be the same person he was back then. You try to avoid him by walking in the other direction; seeing him brings up old self-doubt, and you don't want to experience it again. Tom comes up to you and asks if you have time to talk for a minute. You quickly cross your arms in front of you, preparing to block whatever verbal attack Tom might aim at you. However, Tom throws you a bit of a curveball and apologizes for how he treated you five years ago. *What is happening?* As you try to process this unexpected shift, he tells you he has been through coaching and understands that what he did was wrong. He offers to buy you lunch and wants to rebuild your relationship. You have now placed a new file about Tom in your brain to replace the old one. This new situation becomes the most recent file that will come up when you talk to Tom the next time.

The BASE files are great when they are up to date and serving you. When you use whatever file that comes up without questioning it, though, it can cause issues. The file may be old or corrupt, which can trigger you and cause you to shrink or hide based on old information.

These stories and beliefs are powerful, especially when they are created by a traumatic event. When I coach people, I ask them questions to understand what is holding them back. Why? If we don't uncover what those old BASE files are and create new ones, they will sabotage themselves and their visibility.

If you get a new role but still believe you aren't good enough to have the job, you will sabotage it to get back to a place that is more comfortable for you. Trust your intuition and pay attention to your actions.

BASE File Examples

Here is a list of BASE file examples my clients have shared that relate to their struggles to show value and have confidence. Do any of these resonate for you?

- ☐ I don't feel seen or heard.
- ☐ I remember mistakes and worry about not performing well and disappointing others.
- ☐ I don't stand up for myself or my value.
- ☐ I feel as if I am a failure all the time.
- ☐ I am afraid to take risks and ask for help.
- ☐ I don't set boundaries and don't advocate for myself.
- ☐ I struggle to see my worthiness.

- [ ] I take things personally. Feedback from others causes me to shut down and avoid conversations.
- [ ] I am always comparing myself to others.
- [ ] I fear criticism and self-sabotage to stay safe.
- [ ] I diminish myself and my work.
- [ ] I deflect compliments and recognition.
- [ ] I don't believe in myself.
- [ ] I lack confidence and am unsure what to do to fix it.
- [ ] I tend to put others on a pedestal and defer to leaders who are higher on the organizational chart.
- [ ] I seek external validation instead of trusting myself.
- [ ] I feel as if I am an impostor and people-please too much.

I listed seventeen challenges here. How many apply to you? ....

BASE FILES EXERCISE

What are the top three BASE files that hold you back?

1. ....

    ....

    ....

2. ....

    ....

    ....

Part 2: Foundations for Success

3. ....
....
....

Have you sabotaged any opportunities in your career because they seemed too big and out of your comfort zone?

....
....
....
....
....
....
....
....
....
....
....
....

The interesting thing is that these BASE files are often created when we are young. Until we replace them with something new, they remain in our memories as adults.

Here are my examples:

Old Version: I am judged by the audience whenever I get up to speak in front of a group.
New Version: I am excited to share this information with the audience, and they will learn so much from my speech.

Old Version: I don't belong at the executive table because I don't know enough without an IT degree.
New Version: My business and IT experience in the company give me a great perspective to share with my team and the executives when they talk about new projects and programs.

Like Lori, you don't have to be or have the same skills, qualifications, or experience as everyone else to have value. What do you have that is valuable and helps you stand out?

BASE REPLACEMENTS EXERCISE

Create new versions of your three BASE files that will allow you to play bigger.

1. ....

   ....

   ....

2. ....

   ....

   ....

3. ....

   ....

   ....

Shift how you view your BASE files to focus your time and energy on the positive and avoid self-sabotage. You deserve to take bigger actions to have the career and life that you want! When you get uncomfortable, just recognize that you are about to have a breakthrough. What you're feeling is growth. Don't fight it; focus on learning instead.

Focus on Your Value

You might dismiss things that come easily for you because they seem simple, so you assume everyone can do them. Not true! When someone says you are so good at something, believe them. They are paying you a compliment and admiring what you can do. Say thank you and remember it as one of the valuable gifts you have to offer.

LORI'S VALUE

Based on her belief that she didn't measure up to the lawyers, I knew we needed to focus on helping Lori see her own value and building her confidence back up.

Me: "Lori, can you name all the things you have to offer that would be valuable to the group?"
Lori: "I am process-focused, and my organizational skills, project management, and vision to simplify and improve operations and governance in the company are valuable to the group."

Each week when we met, Lori shared all of her amazing ideas, her vision, strategies that she could implement, and ways she could talk about the value she brought at work.

I remember sitting in my coach's office many years ago, relaying a story about how I handled a situation with my manager at the time. I was taking the blame for something he had done without recognizing it. My coach paused and then said to me, "If you don't value yourself, Sue, why should anyone else value you?"

This one question was worth the whole coaching experience with her. She was right: I wasn't standing up for myself, asking for what I wanted, or challenging others enough. It was so hard to hear, but exactly the feedback that motivated me to do something different.

Slowing down to reflect on my own value was so helpful. I kept trying to fix the opportunities I had instead of embracing the unique outlook, qualities, and skills that made me valuable to the organization. Once I shared more of those things with others and talked about my results and accomplishments, others could see that value. I have seen this happen for my clients as well.

The Value Framework

Before we go on, I want to introduce you to a tool I created to help you build an intentional habit of showing your value. It's called the VALUE Framework, and it will help you focus on being strategic and value driven. You will keep the five steps of the VALUE Framework in mind as you take new actions each week.

The VALUE acronym is simple to remember, but it will take time to learn to operate from a value-driven mindset. To accomplish the visibility outcomes you want, you will need to shift the way you view yourself and let go of some of your old stories and habits. I tell my clients that these actions require intention, consistency, and a willingness to change. I am sharing the VALUE Framework with you so that it becomes part of how you view your opportunities, and so you have this tool to leverage along the rest of your journey.

Part 2: Foundations for Success

Let's walk through it now. I have included an example for you. Each letter of the word VALUE stands for a key word (in bold) that helps you remember to show, talk about, and evaluate your value.

VALUE FRAMEWORK – FOCUS ON VALUE AND IMPACT

FRAME-WORK	DEFINITION	WEEKLY QUESTIONS TO ASK YOURSELF
V	Identify new **Visibility** opportunities.	What opportunities can I leverage for visibility this week?
A	**Amplify** your influence, team, voice and accomplishments.	Who needs to know me or hear about current work, past work, team updates, or new ideas?
L	Use strategic **Language** that tells the story and helps you lead conversations.	What conversations can I lead with influence, impact, and strategic language this week?
U	To help you stand out, leverage what makes you **Unique** and what you are known for.	What can I do to increase my personal brand, gain new experience, and leverage my strengths this week?
E	**Evaluate** your wins, value, impact, and missed opportunities.	How did I add value this week? Did I achieve my VALUE plan? What did I learn to apply to my plan for next week?

Figure 6.1: VALUE Framework - Focus on Value and Impact

Each step of the VALUE Framework feeds into the next to ensure that you are intentional and leveraging the full value of each opportunity. An example plan is included for you on the following page, but if you are process-driven, you might be wondering how to put this together each week. Here is one example approach you can use to prepare your plan. Try different approaches if you want; do what works for you and your style.

SUNDAY EVENING OR MONDAY MORNING:

1. Review your calendar for the week to identify meetings and opportunities that you can leverage for visibility.
2. Use the VALUE Framework template and answer questions to fill in your plan. (Work on the "VALU" steps first and hold off on completing "E" until you get to the end of the week.)

MIDWEEK:

1. Check in on your plan to ensure progress.

AT THE END OF THE WEEK:

1. Evaluate what you did and answer the questions to help you reflect.
2. Create a new plan for the following week.

Turn the page for an example of a leader going through this framework and leveraging meetings and conversations that are already on the calendar.

Your Journey to Visibility Workbook **VALUE** Framework Plan: Week of ....

FRAMEWORK DEFINITION	WEEKLY ACTION PLAN
V - VISIBILITY Identify new Visibility opportunities.	
What opportunities can I leverage for visibility week?	• Three meetings with senior leaders. • Lunch meeting with my mentor on Wednesday. • 1:1 meeting with my manager on Thursday.
A - AMPLIFY Amplify your influence, team, voice, and accomplishments.	
Who needs to know me or hear about current work, past work, team updates, or new work?	• Update senior leaders on the projects in flight and how the team is doing. • Share what I am doing to increase my personal brand with my mentor and ask for support. • Share my updated development plan with my manager and discuss my career.
L - LANGUAGE Use strategic Language that tells the story and helps you lead conversations.	
What conversations can I lead with influence, impact, and strategic language this week?	• Lead the conversations with senior leaders to influence final decisions on funding for phase two. • Discuss with my mentor whom I should build relationships with in the organization. • Ensure that I am clear with my manager on my next career steps and timing.
U - UNIQUE To help you stand out, leverage what makes you Unique and what you are known for.	
What can I do to increase my personal brand, gain new experience, and leverage my strengths this week?	• Ensure that I am showing up boldly and with confidence during my discussions with senior leaders. • Talk to my mentor about other internal or external groups I could leverage my strengths to help. • Share with my manager how I helped the vendor team leverage a negotiation playbook I have used before to ensure consistent messaging.

Showing Value and Building Confidence Foundation

	E - EVALUATE
	Evaluate your wins, value, impact and missed opportunities.

How did I add value this week? Did I achieve my VALUE plan? What did I learn to apply to my plan for next week?	• Helped the senior leaders understand phase two of the projects and secured funding. Also shared examples of where and how I am developing the team by getting them more exposure. Helped the vendor team leverage a negotiation playbook. Shared ideas with my mentor about someone she could meet with to advise her on a challenge she is having. • Did well on the VALUE plan this week and had additional, unplanned conversations with some of my peers. • The plan helped me be more intentional and prepared for conversations. I realized that I forgot to check in on the plan throughout the week to stay on track. I will set a timer on my watch to do a check-in on Wednesday at lunch. I will set up meetings with the contacts that my mentor gave me.

Figure 6.2: Example VALUE Framework Plan

Each step of this plan was considered and intentional, which helped this leader create visibility opportunities and review them from all angles. Other leaders who have tested and implemented this framework shared similar feedback with me. One said, "I have identified so many visibility opportunities that I would have missed otherwise." Another said, "It is helping me focus and be intentional in conversations."

Be consistent with the focused VALUE framework each week. It will boost your visibility in ways you can't imagine and create a value-focused mindset you will carry with you from now on.

Here is a tip: All the things you include in the *E* bucket are what you need to continue to talk about and share with your manager and others in the company. This is your list of wins and results that show your value.

Download the VALUE Framework worksheet at the QR code below so you can complete your weekly review process and increase your visibility.

VALUE EXERCISE

What have you learned by using the weekly VALUE Framework and being intentional about your value?

....

....

....

....

....

....

....

....

....

....

....

....

Be Your Leaders' Equal

Let me clarify what I mean by this. I am not referring to changing the organizational reporting structure. I am only asking you to show up as a thought leader who has the confidence to share your own ideas. Once you view yourself as someone's equal, it changes your confidence and how they see you.

LORI'S OPPORTUNITY TO BE AN EQUAL

As part of her strategy to show her value, Lori needed to demonstrate confidence in a bigger way and show the group she belonged at the table. We walked through her presentation so that she would be prepared. She showed confidence when she spoke, influenced the group with her ideas, and owned her plan. About halfway through our coaching engagement, I asked her, "Did you notice that no one pushed back on anything you wanted to do?" She laughed and said, "I hadn't noticed that, but you're right!" She continued to sell her ideas, get approval to move forward, and gain more confidence each week.

> **COLLABORATION IS VIEWED AS SOMETHING EQUALS DO.**

THE ENDING TO TERESA'S STORY

Do you remember Teresa from Chapter 2, the woman whose site leader kept cutting her off when she spoke up in meetings? I promised to share the end of her story with you. Through the conversations we had about Bob, her site leader, I saw where the issues were for her. Here is a review of her challenges, my advice, and the solutions she implemented.

Challenge 1: Teresa didn't value herself or view herself as Bob's equal, and she wanted Bob to validate her worth.

My advice: Let's focus on what you are doing that is valuable. Bob doesn't need to validate that you are doing good work. Let him come to you if he needs help, not the other way around. Talk about the things that are going well and are valuable to the company. He will be able to hear your value. Let's also get other people singing your praises to him.

Solution 1: Teresa found ways to show her value through feedback from others. She highlighted a major safety issue and was recognized by the company's safety organization. She found ways to improve processes and shared the best practices across all the sites she supported.

Challenge 2: Teresa didn't understand how to communicate strategically with the people in the room and gave too much detail, so Bob cut her off and did not listen to her.

My advice: Make sure the decision-makers are in the meeting. What knowledge do they require in order to decide? What do they believe that isn't true? Can you prepare any of them to support you in advance? We focused heavily on sharing issues and risks from an impact perspective. What will happen if this isn't addressed? What impact will this issue have on the company, team, work, and/or financials if this isn't addressed? What conversations have you already had about solving the problem?

Solution 2: Teresa followed this approach for every update meeting: She gave a brief summary of the issue at hand, what had been done to address it, and conversations she'd had about it already. She offered options to consider, went over potential and actual impacts, and explained what she needed the decision-makers to do (you will learn the Simple Communication Framework that she used in Chapter 9). If Bob cut her off, she stayed as calm as she could and said, "Bob, if we don't discuss and decide on this right now, (insert impact) will happen and none of us want that, correct?"

The way Teresa positioned herself gave her confidence. We practiced minimizing the amount of information she shared in meetings and focused on everything from a value perspective. Her site leader took notice after only a few months of her implementing these changes and started treating her like an equal. Going forward, she could have different conversations about her next role.

Show That You Are An Equal

Taking a more strategic approach and showing up as an equal is crucial to others' perception of you as confident. What you do and the way you position information in conversations creates a narrative about you, and others will create their own narrative about you if you don't do it first. So, what do you want your narrative to be? Do you want to be perceived as someone who needs to be told what to do, or someone who takes the initiative to bring new ideas and solutions to the table?

MICHELLE

Remember Michelle from the introduction? She mentioned in passing that there were some questions she wanted her VP to answer. I asked, "Is there a more strategic way to handle it?"

> Michelle's face reflected her confusion as she replied, "How would I do that?"
>
> I said, "What if you acted as if you were your boss's equal instead of someone who is asking for permission? What would be different in this scenario? Would you still be asking her for answers? What if you said, 'Here are the issues I have identified and solutions I suggest we implement to resolve them. Would love to get your input!'"
>
> We talked about how language and the way you position information tells a story about you. I asked her if she wanted to be perceived as an equal or someone who needs permission. She put her hands on either side her head, spread her fingers wide, and said, "Boom! Of course I want to be seen as an equal."

Here are two key questions you can focus on before you go into a conversation or meeting:

1. What value can I add to this conversation?
2. How can I present my ideas in a way that invites collaboration and showcases my leadership?

How Do You Measure Your Self-Worth and Identity?

In our culture, many believe the only way to have worth is to work hard. The focus is on comparison, external validation, and fitting in, when we should stand out.

We are conditioned this way from an early age, taught to seek approval from family and teachers, adding managers and others as we move into adulthood. So instead of giving ourselves that approval, we seek the prize of high ratings and other feedback that tells us we are doing a good job.

LORI'S SELF-WORTH AND IDENTITY

Lori's job title and the name of her group were decided on by the company before she took the role.

The titles were fine, but they didn't represent her vision. We brainstormed some ideas to help her create a stronger identity to step into along with some ways for the group to demonstrate more value. It would take time for her to sell those changes within the company, but just talking about the possibilities helped her see herself in a bigger way.

Imagine a world where you see your value and are filled with confidence. I want you to trust yourself and show everyone the unique and amazing things you have to offer without reservation. You can do this!

> YOU ARE BORN WORTHY. NO ONE NEEDS TO BESTOW WORTHINESS UPON YOU OR REINFORCE THAT YOU HAVE IT. ACCEPT YOUR SELF-WORTH AND NOTHING WILL TAKE IT AWAY.

When you view yourself as worthy, you show up with confidence. When you identify as less than, you devalue yourself and dismiss anything you do as "not good enough." Here are a few examples:

LOW SELF-WORTH EXAMPLE

Manager: Thanks for all the work you and the team did this weekend!
Low Self-Worth Employee: It was no big deal, no need to thank me. Yes, it was a lot of work, but it is part of our job. I hope the clients find the new program helpful.

HIGH SELF-WORTH EXAMPLE

Manager: Thanks for all the work you and the team did this weekend!
High Self Worth Employee: Thank you for recognizing me and the team. I am so proud of them and all the work they did; it wasn't easy. They went above and beyond to make this program a success! I spoke with our clients, and they are very excited. They will benefit so much from this new program.

Your view of yourself drives all of your actions, behaviors, and the words you use to talk about yourself, your team, and your work. You need to demonstrate confidence in your current role so that leadership can envision you in the next one.

I want to share a special note with anyone who has felt as if their voice didn't matter or was raised to stay in the background. In many cultures, this is the expectation, and being bolder or speaking up may feel as if you are going against long-held family or cultural traditions. It may also stir deeper feelings of discomfort related to acceptance and belonging, or fears of standing out as an outsider. If this is you, I hope you will consider taking some small steps from the workbook to try and move out of your comfort zone.

I understand that this may be uncomfortable and scary for you. Your beliefs tell you that you need to follow the rules you were given. Your voice matters, though, and you have important ideas and perspectives to share. My wish for you is that you believe in yourself enough to embrace who you are and all that you have to offer. I invite you to take at least one small step out of your comfort zone. I understand this is actually a huge deal and a change to your identity, but the reward will be recognition of your own value and letting others see it too! You could be the person who inspires the next generation to speak up, simply because they saw you do it. I hope you will share your voice and thoughts with those who need to hear from you. I believe in you.

Words Matter

I can't stress this enough: Words matter. What you say about yourself, your team, and your work—and how you say it—sends a message to others. Do you project confidence when you speak? Are you someone who confidently demonstrates readiness to take the next step? What is the story you are telling others? What do you want it to be?

· · · · · · · · · · · · · · · · · · · ·

LISTEN TO YOURSELF EXERCISE

I suggest that leaders who aren't sure what narrative they are sharing with others listen carefully to themselves in meetings and presentations. For example, I have clients who ask me to view their recorded presentations and then provide them with feedback. I study how they show up during the presentation or meeting, how they talk about themselves, and the content. I want them to shine, so we discuss what went well and strategize how they can improve for the next time. I recognize how powerful this can be and applaud them for being open to hearing the positives while also receiving constructive feedback. Trust is an important part of this process, and I only want the best for them. There is no judgment here, only opportunities for learning and improvement.

I want to pause here for a moment and share a word of encouragement with anyone who struggles with low self-confidence and fear. You may hesitate to listen to or watch yourself; it might make you feel as uneasy as stepping out on stage with a full audience staring at you. Remember in Chapter 4, when Brad Yates talked about self-sabotage as a form of self-protection? Here are a couple ways to prepare yourself before you watch or listen so that you don't self-sabotage:

1. Be aware that your critical voice will come out in a big way. (Insert your inner critic's name here) will criticize you to protect you from feeling this vulnerable. Remember when I told you about

my inner critic, Victoria? When I go through this exercise myself, I say, "Thank you, Victoria, I appreciate your help, but I want to do this so I can grow and develop." Be grateful that the voice is there to keep you safe and recognize that you may be pulling up old BASE files. This is still your choice to make.

2. If it helps, you can pretend that you are watching your best friend speak and want them to succeed. You wouldn't be mean to your best friend, but you would tell them the truth. This is an opportunity to root for your best friend (aka you) to be successful and learn from the experience. I believe in you. You can do this!

Now that you are prepared, here are three ways to watch or listen to yourself:

- Watch recordings of your presentations.
- Record yourself on your phone while in meetings to hear what you say and how you say it.
- Ask yourself a question that one of your leaders might ask and record your answer as you would deliver it in a meeting.

The goal is to listen compassionately to how you position yourself. Do you demonstrate confidence or not? Note the key words you use that do, and those that devalue or diminish you. For the latter, identify other words to substitute that show you are valuable and worthy of being where you are.

Capture the confident words and phrases you heard yourself use (Yay! Keep using them!):

....

....

....

Showing Value and Building Confidence Foundation

....

....

....

....

Identify words and phrases that devalue you and your work or sound negative:

....

....

....

....

....

....

What positive, confident words and phrases do you want to exchange for the devaluing or negative ones?

....

....

....

....

....

....

What did you learn about yourself by doing this exercise?

....

....

....

....

....

Self-Trust Is Key

Self-trust is one of the keys to being a successful leader. It helps you make the right decisions based on your experience, intuition, and the data and facts available to you. A leader who believes in themselves shows up with confidence. Team members want to work for you when you make confident decisions, have a vision, and develop your team. Your ability to leverage your unique experiences and perspective, and trust yourself, will automatically make you stand out as a leader.

LORI'S OPPORTUNITY TO DEMONSTRATE SELF-TRUST

A big goal of Lori's was to transform her function. She identified what would make the biggest impact on the company and came up with a plan. Her idea would bring a standardized and more productive approach to the work, a single location for storing things, and greater efficiency through the use of AI tools. She knew that there had been issues adopting such tools in the past and she would get pushback, but it didn't deter her from trusting herself and moving this huge transformation forward. No matter the obstacle, she overcame it and continued down

> her chosen path. She got the whole company into alignment behind her plan (not an easy feat), gained funding approval, and moved forward to execute the plan. She trusted herself through every challenge that came her way.

Leaders need a perspective that is grounded in their beliefs and values and demonstrates confidence in their vision. Without self-trust, this can be tough to have in place. Those who lack self-trust are too focused on what everyone else wants and don't take the time to listen to themselves. Too many other opinions get in the way of their best decision-making.

SELF-TRUST EXERCISE

Take five minutes with no distractions and consider a problem or issue you need to solve. Listen to yourself, decide what you want to do, and note your answer here. (Do not ask for anyone else's opinion until you are clear on your own answer.)

....

....

....

....

....

....

....

Be Your Own Advocate

Do you speak about your accomplishments with others, or do you hope your manager will do it for you? I made a bad assumption at one point in my career, believing my manager had communicated something when she hadn't. I had to have a hard conversation with my VP, who said, "You need to advocate for yourself and your team instead of relying on your manager to do it for you. Your manager can still do it, but it is better if you are in the room and do it yourself." It was a good lesson for me to learn, and I never let someone else speak for me again. When I coach leaders, I want them to learn how to advocate for themselves, including with their management. When they do that, it automatically creates opportunities for others to talk about their own work.

LORI'S SELF-ADVOCACY

At the end of our coaching, Lori told me, "Do you remember when I told you that I didn't belong in the room when we first started working together? Everything we have worked on has changed how I see myself, and the way I show up has changed how people see me. I go into meetings and ask for what I need to ensure that a program is successful. I no longer feel that I don't belong in the room. I walked into a meeting the other day and told myself, *I own the room!*" How amazing is that? Lori went from low confidence and feeling like she didn't fit in to feeling confident and self-assured. She not only believes that she belongs in the room now, but she also knows she owns it!

Be your own messenger so that what you are doing comes from you directly. You can't assume that your manager shares what you do or will help you get the job you want. They may not be good at sharing their ideas or accomplishments, either. You need to take the lead and share what you and your team have done. Each time you do, you can use it as an opportunity to build your relationship with the leadership team or other influencers in the organization.

SELF-ADVOCACY EXERCISE

Where do you have an opportunity to advocate for yourself, and when will you do it?

....

....

....

....

....

....

....

....

Key Learnings

This was a long chapter, but one of the most important for you to work through. Seeing your value and having confidence are critical to your success. It's okay if you aren't all the way there yet; keep working on the exercises in this chapter. Keep focusing on your VALUE Framework and you will notice a difference. I have coached hundreds of leaders on how to do this and if you want to be visible, this is the way forward. Nothing is more important than for you to see your own value, trust yourself, and advocate for what you want. Leaders who embrace the value they bring show up with confidence, and that changes how everyone else views them. It's time for you to capture your key learnings about your value and confidence from this chapter!

PART 3

ASSESS CHALLENGES AND TAKE ACTION

Assess your challenges, choose your solution paths, and take bigger actions to increase your visibility, value, and impact.

Chapter 7
STEP 4: ASSESS—WHAT PATH IS BEST FOR YOU?

Inside Chapter 7

The objective of this chapter is to take you through an assessment of the various visibility challenges you may be facing. Each challenge category includes example language (from real clients) that you can read through to determine if it is similar to what you experience. The sum of scores by challenge category, based on your assessment results, will provide insight into what you may want to consider focusing on first. Let's take the "assess" step and answer the fourth question on your journey to greater visibility: "What path is best for you?"

Preparing for The Visibility Challenges Assessment

Reflect on what you have learned over the last three chapters as you prepare to assess yourself:

- Are there patterns or rules that you have been following for a long time and are ready to change?
- Where are you holding yourself back from showing up in a bigger way?
- What feedback have you received that will impact whether you will be considered for future roles and opportunities?
- What do you need to start working on now to achieve the desired future you defined in Chapter 3?

Part 3: Assess Challenges and Take Action

Taking the Visibility Challenges Assessment

Each path has fifteen examples to review. Go through each challenge path and place an X next to each example that resonates with you.

PATH ONE – COMMUNICATION / CLARITY CHALLENGES

☐ I don't know how to communicate strategically with the executive level.

☐ I don't know how to communicate succinctly and clearly.

☐ I want to increase my confidence so I can communicate better and verbalize what needs to be said.

☐ I struggle to show up for and initiate difficult conversations.

☐ I don't know how to lead conversations.

☐ I struggle to find clarity amidst the chaos of change.

☐ I am unable to think on my feet.

☐ I tend to share everything and am not framing conversations strategically.

☐ I don't know how to use data to share valuable insights.

☐ I don't know how to articulate my value to others.

☐ I communicate with a focus on specific tasks vs. using strategic language.

☐ My pace and style of communication are very different from those of the people I present to.

☐ It is difficult for me to voice how I feel. I feel like I am alone in this struggle.

☐ I avoid conflict and don't challenge others.

☐ I avoid opportunities to present in front of groups.

PATH TWO – INFLUENCING / RELATIONSHIP CHALLENGES

- [ ] I am not building relationships with influencers at all.
- [ ] I am not viewed as a strategic influencer who makes an impact.
- [ ] I want to influence others and sell my ideas, but I don't know how.
- [ ] I want to be able to influence others even when I don't have authority.
- [ ] I am afraid to meet with influencers because I don't know what to say.
- [ ] I don't know how to maintain ongoing relationships with senior leaders and influencers.
- [ ] I am not getting in front of mentors and sponsors on a regular basis.
- [ ] I am not viewed as a trusted resource by teams and management.
- [ ] I don't share updates about myself or my team with management.
- [ ] I don't talk about my accomplishments or ask for what I want.
- [ ] I am not doing enough to gain recognition for my work and my team.
- [ ] I don't manage up with (communicate effectively and stay aligned with, support) my manager.
- [ ] I don't leverage my peer relationships to collaborate and learn.
- [ ] I don't have strong relationships with my clients or leaders in other parts of the organization.
- [ ] My senior leadership team doesn't know me or what I do.

PATH THREE – LEADING / BEING STRATEGIC CHALLENGES

- [ ] I don't see myself as a leader who thinks bigger and broader and creates the future.
- [ ] I don't know how to quickly gain respect and establish authority.

Part 3: Assess Challenges and Take Action

☐ I am too busy and need to find more time to slow down and think.

☐ I know I should be more visible but I'm not sure where to begin.

☐ I want to enable team members' success and build their exposure.

☐ I don't take on opportunities for projects that would give me exposure.

☐ I am afraid to trust and delegate to my team.

☐ I don't know how to deal with ambiguity, and I am afraid to make decisions.

☐ I am not perceived as a strong leader.

☐ I don't know how to help my remote team become more visible.

☐ I want to move from the background and participate with executives as a strategic thinker.

☐ I do my team's jobs for them.

☐ My team can't operate without me.

☐ I am tentative in my responses and usually ask for permission or approval.

☐ I struggle to focus on high-value activities.

Challenge Category Summary

Count the number of examples that resonated with you in each of the challenge paths and enter those numbers in the table below:

PATHS	PATH ONE Communication / Clarity Challenges	PATH TWO Influencing / Relationship Challenges	PATH THREE Leading / Being Strategic Challenges
Example Totals			

What Path Is Best for You?

The path with the highest number indicates that you should focus your efforts there first. In Chapter 8, I will introduce you to the three different solution paths that will show you how to take the next step in your journey with the information you have gained through the assessment.

Key Takeaways

What did you learn in this chapter by taking the assess step to answer, "What path is best for you?" that will help you achieve greater visibility? Note your primary path to focus on in the next chapter.

....

....

....

....

....

....

....

....

....

....

....

....

....

Part 3: Assess Challenges and Take Action

Chapter 8
STEP 5: TAKE ACTION—WHAT PATH DO YOU CHOOSE?

CONGRATULATIONS! YOU MADE IT THROUGH the Visibility and Career Growth Framework and the Foundations for Success, and now it's time for action! You have reflected, answered questions, and focused on what you need to do to be more visible. This work is challenging. But now comes the fun part! You are ready to take all the things you learned about yourself and show what you can do.

This is the time to focus on the nuances of what you say and do, and how you position yourself in front of your leadership or others you are trying to influence. The work you will do throughout the rest of this workbook will change you and transform how others see you. It is now time to complete the "take action" step and answer the last question on your journey to greater visibility: "What path do you choose?"

The Creation of the Solution Paths

An initial coaching session with a potential client is focused on what coaches call "discovery." This is when the coach listens to the client's challenges, the language they use to describe their struggles, and what they hope to gain from coaching. I may learn some things in discovery, but I never assume I have the whole story. I follow up with tougher questions to uncover what is happening beneath the surface. If a client is unaware that their BASE files have taken over, they won't be able to make the shifts necessary for change.

As a coach, I have leaned on my intuition on more than one occasion after a discovery session to help guide a client toward a particular path, and this has worked well. The client follows the path, works through mindset shifts, takes action, and gains confidence. That sounds so simple, but it takes work to make these changes and show up differently. It has been such an honor to partner with so many amazing leaders who once operated with doubt and fear but now believe in themselves and show their value to others. I want that for you too.

I have shared frameworks, resources, and examples to prepare you for it; now I will give you the "secret sauce" that I use when coaching clients. The solution paths in the next three chapters have what you need to act and achieve greater visibility. You can pick and choose what you want to implement based on tried-and-true solutions and the results of your assessment in Chapter 7.

When I put the solution paths together, I focused on you and the challenges you face each day. I have faced them, too, and so have my clients. Although I am not there in person to support you, you can trust that I am giving you everything you need to meet those challenges. You will have to be brave, ready to step out of your comfort zone, and resilient in order to keep going when it would be easier to just stay where you are. Remember, you have the agency to make choices no matter what. I can lay out these paths for you, but I can't walk them for you. This is your choice. Do you want to settle for what you have right now or go after a bigger future (look at the future state vision you laid out in Chapter 3? No need to wait any longer. Let's make it happen!

Inside the Solution Paths

You have been in the shallow end of the pool up until now. It's time to swim in the deep end and show yourself (and everyone else) that you belong there.

I remember holding on for dear life to the side of the pool at the local YMCA in the town where I grew up, waiting for the final test in beginner swimming when I was about six or seven years old. I told myself, *You HAVE to let go and swim across the deep end, everyone is watching and waiting for you!* Have you ever tried to swim when every part of your body is completely tensed up? It doesn't work very well. I was scared to let go for fear that I would simply sink to the bottom. Some people take to swimming as if they are ducks; I am not one of them. I had to work hard at swimming, and the experience was similar when I went through my journey to visibility.

Challenging your BASE files is as scary as exploring the deep end of the pool. When you take that brave first action of letting go, you will learn that the fear, although uncomfortable, actually makes you stronger. You will prove to yourself that you can do it. (In case you are wondering, I did pass the swimming test, but let's just say I am way better at visibility than I am at swimming.)

Each of the solution paths reflects how I work with clients to help them address that specific set of challenges. Read the case studies, scripts to follow, ways to reframe your thinking and language, examples from real life scenarios, templates to use, and methods for tracking progress. The outcome for each path is built to help you shift how you see yourself and your language and focus on value-based actions.

If you are leveraging the VALUE Framework from Chapter 6, you should be seeing lots of opportunities now that were not clear to you before. Giving you the VALUE Framework in Chapter 6 was intentional. I wanted you to start seeing those opportunities and begin to take advantage of them. Now you can take them to the next level and show others your value.

It's All About Your Mindset

Remember Sheri, my friend the big adventurer who appeared in the introduction? If you are like her, you will view this part of the workbook as a fun exploration. Your travel to each of the solution paths offers you an opportunity to "choose your own adventure." As you explore the options, you will build your action plan to include what resonates with you and tackles your specific challenges. Get excited about learning and implementing new actions! The shifts you make will be overt in some cases and subtle in others, but they will definitely change how you are perceived.

SARAH

When Sarah came to work with me, she had left her last company a few months before and was struggling to find a new role. She was holding onto some old beliefs about herself and her capabilities from her previous role. During our first coaching session, she said, "I'm feeling lost and confused—I have no idea what I want to do or how to move forward." Still, she came in motivated and ready to do the work. We used to joke that she got an *A* for doing her homework. After working together for six months on her specific solution paths, she wrote, "I have more confidence and understand what I have to offer an employer now. Sue helped me focus on how I wanted to show up in my new job and what I wanted to accomplish. I gained more confidence and visibility in every aspect of my life." Investing in yourself and doing the work will help you achieve your goal too.

Choosing Your Path

It's time to decide on the solution path that is best for you. Let's start with the challenge path that you scored the highest on in the last chapter. You may want to check out that path first, but choosing a different path is perfectly fine too. There is no requirement to go in a specific order. This is the time to use the choose-your-own-adventure option, so have fun with it!

Your next steps are to select your primary challenge path from Chapter 7 based on the outcome of your assessment (or choose another if you want), select the solution path that matches your challenge path, and create your action plan. You will find your action plan template included in the resources page at the end of each solution path chapter.

CHALLENGE(S) ⇨ SOLUTION PATH(S) ⇨ CREATE YOUR ACTION PLAN

Chapters 9 through 11 are each dedicated to a specific path so you can take a deeper dive and get plenty of practical approaches to these challenges.

To go directly to the solution paths, here are the chapter numbers.

COMMUNICATION / CLARITY SOLUTION PATH – CHAPTER 9

INFLUENCING / RELATIONSHIP SOLUTION PATH – CHAPTER 10

LEADING / BEING STRATEGIC SOLUTION PATH – CHAPTER 11

Solution Path Set-Up

At the beginning of each solution path chapter, you will find:

- A story or case study that encompasses the focus of that solution path.
- Clear headlines showing what that section includes (e.g., examples, reflection questions, templates, and frameworks to use.

At the end of each solution path chapter, you will find:

- A quick recap of that chapter's focus areas and reflection questions.

- A QR code that lets you access your action plan template, plus additional resources including podcasts and videos. (You can also see an example of the action plan template in the appendix.)

Since I have it too, I know that your overachiever mindset is ready to jump into the pool with both feet (to continue our swimming metaphor) and try to do everything quickly. However, there is no rush to complete any or all of the paths. The goal here is to slow down, be intentional, and identify new opportunities to demonstrate your skills. Give yourself the time and space to hold onto the side of the pool for a minute so you can get used to the new you. It takes time to bring these  new skills to who you are and how you show up. Taking it slow is an important part of the process and will keep you from sabotaging your progress by going back to those old, comfortable BASE files. The new files are so much better for you and will help you transform your visibility and your leadership!

Key Takeaways

What did you learn in this chapter by taking the last action step and answering, "What path do you choose?" that will help you achieve greater visibility?

....

....

....

....

....

What Path Do You Choose?

Chapter 9
THE COMMUNICATION / CLARITY SOLUTION PATH

I HAVE FOUND ONE THING to be true in this work: you don't need to change who you are, but you do need to use different words to show the value you bring. Let me unpack what that means for you.

Clients will bring up situations in which they need and want to communicate, but their approach to these conversations often lacks strategy and originality. What I ask them to do is communicate in a way that sets them apart. Now I want to help you to do this too. How can you differentiate yourself and show the value you have to offer so you get the opportunities you want?

> **STEVE'S STORY**
>
> "I need your help."
>
> These were the first words Steve said to me when we got on a call after yet another difficult client meeting. Steve was a director with potential, but he struggled in one area of his leadership: He was unable to communicate with clients in a way that demonstrated his value or helped them follow his messaging. This was preventing him from getting alignment within the company and making it hard for him to move his projects forward. He was a

strong technical leader but couldn't get his recommendations across to clients successfully. His manager told him that he gave too much detail, started conversations without enough context, and jumped around too much during presentations for clients to follow the thread. Sometimes technical language can be challenging and hard to follow. However, Steve's issues had nothing to do with being too technical; the problem was, he wasn't doing what he needed to do up front to align with the people he was trying to communicate with. I call this "taking people on the journey with you," and I will show you what it means in practice in the next section.

Preparing for a Conversation

You may be saying to yourself, *Why do I need to prepare for a conversation?* It was one of my challenges too. I would get into the room and forget what I wanted to say, or ramble along while hoping that my point was coming through okay. I didn't always consider that more context or relevant examples would help others understand me better. My tendency (due to nerves, since I didn't practice in advance) was to jump into conversations without context, which of course caused confusion for the other parties. I also jumped back and forth between key points, making it even harder to follow me and chipping away at their confidence in me and what I was sharing. I had to learn how to present in a better way.

REFLECTION QUESTION

How do you prepare for a conversation?

HELPING STEVE PREPARE FOR NEW CONVERSATIONS

Everyone gives me pushback when I talk about preparing for conversations, citing a lack of time, and Steve was no different. I shared my own stories of going into client and senior leadership conversations with little or no preparation and my similarly poor outcomes, then asked him if he would be open to trying what had worked for me and my clients. He nodded yes. I said, "Would you ever put a new system into production without testing it?" He shook his head in an emphatic no, just as I expected. "An important presentation or conversation is just like a new application system," I explained. "You need to 'test' what you want to say in advance to help you get ready and show up stronger in the moment." Although we were on a virtual video call, Steve leaned forward in anticipation of what I would say next. He had connected the dots with what he knew from the technical world and understood what I meant by being prepared.

I walked him through the VALUE Framework from Chapter 6 first and asked him to identify his big visibility opportunities for the week. He had two key meetings coming up with both systems and business leadership. Then we went through the key preparation questions (on the next page) to help him come up with ideas. He filled in the rest of the framework worksheet and captured the key points he needed to communicate in the meeting. I asked him to share with me how he would say them, and we practiced ways for him to state them more succinctly and use language to demonstrate thought leadership. Steve's before and after results are in the next section.

Part 3: Assess Challenges and Take Action

CONVERSATION PREPARATION EXERCISE

Here are the key questions I used to ask myself when preparing for various professional conversations. You can select the questions that work best for you.

- [ ] What outcome do I want?
- [ ] What is the story and message I want to communicate?
- [ ] Do I need to provide background on this topic?
- [ ] What are all the things I need to say to get the message across?
- [ ] What information do I have about the person/people I plan to talk with and what is important to them?
- [ ] How can I say it so they will receive it in the best possible way?
- [ ] What objections will they have that I can address proactively?
- [ ] What questions can I ask to better understand the situation?
- [ ] What might I be assuming that could be wrong?
- [ ] What should I include in the conversation about me, my team, or our work that they are unaware of and will show my impact?
- [ ] Have I shared what I want to do in my career clearly and with the right people, and has anything changed that I now need to communicate?
- [ ] Have I communicated to the influencers what my team and I are doing so they can support us?

Answering these questions in advance will demonstrate that you have done your homework and have a plan for the conversation. When you have clarity, it is easier for the other person to follow your message, and that helps you get what you need out of the conversation.

What questions in the previous list will help you prepare for your own conversations?

....

....

....

....

....

....

....

....

....

....

Once I started planning for my conversations in advance, they improved dramatically. I knew what I wanted to accomplish and what stories I wanted to tell. Other people could easily follow what I was saying when I used examples that pertained to them. It was worth it to plan in advance, and it helped me get to the outcomes I needed and wanted.

The Simple Communication Framework (SCF)

This framework is great to use for presentations or in one-on-one meetings or interviews. I learned about the importance of communicating strategically when under pressure during my time at Kraft. Unexpected situations, such as being asked to present at the last minute or provide an answer quickly, cropped up all the time. Following this type of simple framework is a great way to ensure group alignment and that everyone can journey through the discussion together. This approach also keeps you from straying too far from the planned conversation and enables everyone to follow along so you get what you need!

REFLECTION QUESTION

How will you ensure that everyone is on the same page at the beginning of your meetings?

STEVE WAS READY TO USE THE NEW FRAMEWORK

I knew this tool would to be a game changer for Steve, who tended to start in the middle of conversations without aligning everyone first. Following the Simple Communication Framework would keep him organized and allow everyone else to follow his message so he could get what he needed from the discussion.

Start with an executive summary of what you are presenting, following this format:

- Introduce the topic that you will share.
- Highlight three things that you will discuss.
- Share what you expect from the person or group by the end of the meeting.

The Communication / Clarity Solution Path

Add details of the conversation or presentation:

- Share the context of the topic that you want to discuss (like a project, program, idea, or issue) to ensure that everyone is on the same page and in case anyone has missed a meeting.
- Talk about three things pertaining to the topic (like options, ideas, recommendations, or issues). Provide some details, but not so many that you lose the audience. The "threes approach" makes it easy for you to remember what you want to share and easy for others to hear.
- The final step is to ask for what you need from the decision-makers (for example, make a decision, get approval or feedback, or plan another meeting.

Here is an example of an executive summary I could have included in a presentation to a leadership team when I worked at Kraft:

> "I am here today to present an update on the Master Data Global Program. This update will include the global team's current status, a budget vs. actuals review, and an overview of the next phase planned for the regions. The team needs you to provide a decision about the next phase of the program at the end of the discussion today."

Obviously, this example is much shorter than a true presentation. The goal is for you to learn how to be succinct with the information, talk about it in terms of facts that are easy to follow, and show credibility. You will have prepared the group for what will be covered and where you need their help at the beginning of the presentation so that they will pay attention. They want you to communicate with value and confirm that everything is under control.

Part 3: Assess Challenges and Take Action

Senior leaders have little time to waste. You need to be prepared to share the journey of your topic in order to bring everyone along with you and in case people haven't been in every meeting. You also need to proactively address questions and show that you have a handle on things. Presenting in meetings is a great way to gain visibility for yourself and your team.

YOUR SCF (Simple Communication Framework) SCRIPT EXERCISE

What would you put into the script for a presentation or conversation that you need to have soon?

Summary/Context/Topic:

....

....

....

....

....

....

Three Things About the Topic:

1. ....

2. ....

3. ....

The Communication / Clarity Solution Path

What is needed? (What outcome do you need or want?)

....

....

....

....

....

Be Strategic and Succinct

Imagine that you are in a meeting with your peers and leadership team. You want to contribute to the conversation and share your ideas, but you are concerned about what to say. In my own past experience, I would go into a small panic in this moment. I wanted to make sure that what I said came across in the right way, but you can't come up with anything coherent when you are in panic mode!

> **REFLECTION QUESTION**
> *What can you do to get ready to share*
> *your thoughts in a meeting?*

STEVE'S SHIFT TO BE MORE STRATEGIC AND SUCCINCT

In Steve's previous role as doer in his group, more technical detail was expected; but now he was leading a team and needed to communicate at a higher level. These conversations were out of his comfort zone, but he was ready to make the change and show up as a leader who understood both the technical and business sides of the company. He knew that this was an opportunity to leverage the Simple Communication Framework instead of approaching things as he had in the past. He didn't want to freeze. Most of all, he wanted to demonstrate that he was acting on the feedback he had received.

Here are Steve's before and after examples:

Before: "The reporting system we use needs an upgrade. I talked to the vendor about it, and we went through different options. We will need to make technical changes to perform the upgrade. I reviewed the options and the one I chose will cost a lot of money. This needs to be done ASAP. We will have to take the system down for the next two weekends in order to get the backup done and the upgrade completed."

There are a lot of open questions here. I asked Steve to tell me what his clients asked him; he went through a whole list of questions.

- "You are asking us to make decisions with little to no information. What is driving the urgency here?"
- "If the system needs an upgrade, how come I am just hearing about it now?"
- "What are the options, and are there more cost-effective choices?"
- "You are telling me we have to go down over the next two weekends, but what is the risk with all of these changes? What is your contingency plan?"
- "How urgent is this upgrade, and what is the risk if we wait?"
- "What do we tell our users?"

The Communication / Clarity Solution Path

This situation did not build credibility for Steve, and he was embarrassed. He was fully aware that he had shared information with no plan and that he no longer wanted to deliver presentations or enter discussions that way. Here is what we came up with and practiced using the SCF approach.

After: "Let me share why we are here today. The purpose of this meeting is to discuss a system upgrade that we need to do soon. I want to discuss the options and risk factors so you can make the best decision.

The system went down multiple times over the last few days, and it has caused everyone to have issues with access. When we spoke with the vendor, they told us that we are out of support for this version and need to do an upgrade. This was a complete surprise, but we found out it had been communicated to someone on the team; however, they assumed it was an automated upgrade and that they didn't need to do anything. I have explained to that person how to handle any communication on upgrades in the future.

I will go through the three upgrade options I have put together with the vendor's help to show you the costs, the down time, the risk factors, and the communications approach. With the system going down frequently, we will need to decide as soon as possible. If we can do that today it would be great, but if you need more time, we can reconnect tomorrow. We can't wait any longer than that to decide."

What are the differences? In the new example, Steve has a well-planned out approach. He starts with context, provides the important details to enable decision-making, owns the issues that have occurred, and enables a better understanding of what

> the options are moving forward. This builds Steve's leadership's confidence in him as a leader who can handle a crisis situation calmly and put together a plan to solve it.

Here is an easy way to stay out of panic mode and in prepared mode for any meeting.

PRE-MEETING CHECK-IN EXERCISE

Identify an upcoming meeting. What is on the agenda, and what might come up in the meeting for you to comment on?

....

....

....

....

....

....

....

....

....

....

....

The Communication / Clarity Solution Path

What are three questions you could ask about the meeting topics?

1. ....

   ....

2. ....

   ....

3. ....

   ....

Is there something you need to bring up to the group for discussion?

....

....

....

....

....

Using the pre-meeting check-in prior to your meetings helps you create thoughtful questions and responses instead of trying to come up with them in the moment.

Reframing Conversations

You might assume that the conversations you are having with stakeholders are good right now, but are you visible compared to others in the room? What if you could take a simple conversation, reframe it, and make it stand out?

In addition, you have so many opportunities for this outside of in-person meetings and conversations to consider, like emails, presentations, and information that you might share via collaborative software. Are you using language to show the value of what you are doing? Take the extra step to explain how the things you have done will make an impact on the business, the company, and your team. This is what will show that you are strategic, and differentiate you from everyone else.

REFLECTION QUESTION

When you have conversations with stakeholders, do they show the value and impact that you are making?

STEVE'S OPPORTUNITY TO REFRAME CONVERSATIONS

Steve brought in some examples of what he had been sharing with his management. To start, we reviewed some of his status updates and emails to identify what he had included or missed. I explained the concept of reframing communication to show more value and impact. I continued to reinforce that there was nothing wrong with what he had shared, but that it could be so much more powerful with some reframing. As we went through these communications, I used a few of them to show him what the reframed version would be.

Example Number One: Status Update for Management

Here are before and after examples of one of Steve's email updates to his manager. Notice the language that is used in each, how they are framed, and how the revised version shows his value as a leader.

Original Version: "The team finished the project yesterday and we are starting on the new one."

Value Focused Version: "This project was an opportunity for me to fully delegate to the team to execute. The team did an incredible job of working out the final issues and pulling together to finish the project on time yesterday. I was so proud of them! We got great feedback from the clients! I am giving John the opportunity to lead this new project. He is ready for more responsibility and this project will help him to demonstrate his skills as a leader."

What are the differences between the two?

- The original version is simply information without much context. It does not show any value, nor does it answer any additional questions Steve's manager might have.
- The value-focused version provides more visibility into what had to happen for the project to be completed. It also shows how Steve delegated and his team pulled together and finished on time. This example demonstrates clarity, focus on strategy, and that Steve was developing his team by giving one of them the exposure to try something new.

Remember, you are the person who creates the narrative, sets the tone, and influences others' opinions of you and your team. Anyone can write the original version, but the leader who writes the value-focused version stands out.

The language you use and the information you offer to others about the work you and your team are doing are what will create the perception of your group. If a tough decision needs to be made about who to eliminate from an organization, the groups who don't show their value will be the first ones to be considered. That is why it is so important to learn how to share information in a way that helps you, your team, and your contributions become more visible.

Example Number Two: Email to the Director

Original Version: "You asked me to put together the first draft of the presentation and a list of questions for our client meeting next week. I did the best I could but am not sure what else to include. Can you help me write them?"

Value Focused Version: "Here is the presentation and a list of questions I put together for the client meeting next week. I asked for input from the team to ensure that we included all the scenarios. The presentation slides are ready to go and include the options, analysis, and recommendations for the meeting. Do you have any input to add?"

What are the differences between the two?

The original version portrays someone who is seeking permission and shows that Steve is reliant on his manager to do his job. If Steve's director needs to write the presentation and the questions, they don't need Steve. That sounds harsh, but the goal is to add value. Therefore, Steve must be mindful of what he does and says to show his value to his manager and others in the organization. He now knows that he must take the initiative to figure things out and only get their help as an exception, after he has tried everything else first. The value-focused version shows his confidence in and ownership of the work. Steve did his due diligence, gathered input, and created the presentation with all the analysis and recommendations. He only asked if there is anything to add from his director's perspective.

REFRAMING CONVERSATIONS EXERCISE

Review some of your own emails to identify where you could reframe them to show more value and impact. Write down what you noticed when reviewing the sent emails and how you reframed the new versions.

....

....

....

....

....

....

....

....

....

....

....

Weaving in Value and Impact

How many times have you walked by someone in the hall or been in a meeting with them but didn't want to bother them with what you had to share? I can't tell you how many times I talked myself out of sharing things because I didn't want to "bother" anyone!" What if the other person valued what you had to share? If you include value, the conversation will be viewed as valuable.

> **REFLECTION QUESTION**
> *What opportunities do you have to say more about your skills, results, and what makes you unique in conversation?*

> **HOW STEVE MADE THE SHIFT TO VALUE AND IMPACT**
>
> I asked Steve to describe what was different for him after viewing these examples. He said, "I heard you say the words value and impact, but I didn't get what you meant until you showed me. I can definitely recognize the difference this will make for me to get my ideas across." I asked him to create a list of two or three things he would add to his VALUE Framework sheet to share with others. Now he had what he needed to take advantage of visibility opportunities.

Do you have a list of accomplishments, plans, or ideas that you want to share? Are you taking advantage of opportunities to share them?

CREATING OPPORTUNITIES EXERCISE – PART 1

What are two things you need to share with your boss, a peer, or one of your direct reports that you haven't had time for yet?

1. ....

....

....

2. ....

....

....

Have you ever been in a situation where you minimized your work or your team's so you wouldn't be seen as a braggart? Unfortunately, I did this way too often. My favorite sayings used to be "It was no big deal" and "Just doing my job." I would say these things about huge programs that took multiple years to implement. Learn from my mistakes.

Please read the next sentence and view it as me strongly encouraging you:

> **WHAT YOU DO IS A BIG DEAL AND YOU SHOULD ABSOLUTELY TELL PEOPLE WHAT YOU DO, HOW IT ADDS VALUE, AND HOW IT MAKES AN IMPACT ON THE COMPANY!**

Every interaction is an opportunity for visibility, so don't let them go by without taking advantage of that. Speak in facts and you won't be seen as a braggart, just someone who is sharing information.

Part 3: Assess Challenges and Take Action

For example, let's say John and Paul meet in the hallway at work.

> John could walk by and say, "Hi, Paul, how's it going?" without stopping.
>
> What if instead, John said, "Paul, I am so glad I ran into you! I wanted to thank you and your team for your support on our project. We were able to implement it quickly and we couldn't have done it without your partnership. I'll make sure your team gets recognized for their work!"

Let's use John and Paul in a separate example.

> John is busy and barely acknowledges that Paul is walking past him. He keeps going to get to his next meeting.
>
> Instead, John could say, "Hey, Paul! Great work on the ABC project you just completed! I am late for a meeting but would love to have lunch next week to talk more about it if you have time." Paul responds, "Thanks so much, I appreciate it! I will find time on your calendar and set it up for us."

Sharing a more valuable message takes less than thirty seconds and helps the other person feel valued and seen. Great leaders understand the value in relationships and take the time to have conversations.

The Communication / Clarity Solution Path

Mary is in her new finance role and wants to make a great impression the first time she meets Diane, a supply chain VP who is her client. Using this simple introduction template, Mary introduces herself first:

Hi, my name is (name) and I am the (your title) in (insert your department or group). I have (number) years of experience in (industry/company), where I've held leadership roles in (enter types of roles/functions that you have been in to show your experience). I am known for (or I am passionate about, I love to focus on) (enter things here that would set you apart from others and use active verbs like transforming, creating, turning things around, changing, or disrupting).

Here is Mary's version:

"Hi, my name is Mary. I am the new finance director here at the company. I have ten years of experience in consumer product goods finance at two other companies where I held leadership roles supporting supply chain, IT, procurement, and sales. My focus in all of my roles has been on transformation and finding innovative ways to enable faster business decisions through financial data. I'm originally from the Chicago area and moved to Dallas five years ago with my husband and three kids."

This kind of introduction can be sent in an email or shared verbally. It seems formal when written, but you can include whichever parts you want and make it much more conversational when you say it. Add anything else that is pertinent to the conversation or the person you are meeting. You are building a connection with the other person and sharing information so that they will remember you.

Once Mary is in the meeting, she can share something similar to the following:

"Thank you for meeting with me today. Diane, my manager, suggested that we meet since I will be supporting your team now. I would love to learn about your role and the projects that your team is working on, share a little about my background, and agree on the best way for us to work together going forward."

Do you see how the Simple Communication Framework from earlier in the chapter was used here? (You could also send this short paragraph in advance, as an email.)

During the conversation, listen carefully to what the other person says and ask thoughtful questions. Show that you are coming in with experience and understand their challenges. Don't assume anything. Until you are sure, stay open and keep these things in mind:

- Are there gaps, challenges, or other things you could potentially help with or support them in?
- Leverage examples and results you had in previous companies or roles when going through your background. Share what you will be working on now and be open to answering questions.
- What might resonate the best with this person to show them the value you bring to your role and their team?
- Remember the questions for conversation prep from earlier in this chapter? Planning your conversations can be helpful.
- Keep notes after the meeting and follow up in a future meeting as you learn more.

CREATING OPPORTUNITIES EXERCISE – PART 2

To show added value, what would you change about the two things you wrote down in Part 1 of this exercise?

1. ....

   ....

2. ....

   ....

Difficult Conversations

Difficult conversations don't happen for many reasons. Are you someone who is conflict-avoidant, lacks enough confidence to discuss the situation, is afraid it won't make a difference, or fears that you will be judged or criticized if it doesn't go well? All the other stories we make up in our heads get in the way of conversations that could provide win-wins for all. Imagine if everyone went into difficult conversations assuming the best outcome. Wouldn't that clear up so many issues?

REFLECTION QUESTION
What has prevented you from having difficult conversations?

STEVE'S DIFFICULT CONVERSATION

Steve seemed distracted when we got on our call. I asked him what was going on. He said, "Remember the difficult client that I meet with quarterly? Our call is coming up in the next two weeks and I can't have the same experience with him that I did last time." I reminded him how much he had been doing to shift his communication during the previous months. "How can you create a different experience with this client this time?" I asked. Steve began to walk through all the steps and capture what he would do for each one. He asked me a few questions throughout his process. I watched his shoulders relax, and he was visibly calmer by the time he finished.

IS THE DIFFICULT CONVERSATION NECESSARY? EXERCISE

Ask yourself the following questions when you need to decide if you should have a difficult conversation. Remember, you can't change other people. You can influence them to come around to your point of view, but it may not change their decision. Sometimes you have to agree to disagree. Answer the questions below about the difficult situation you have been avoiding.

Is the conflict within you, and the other person has no idea why you are upset?

....

....

....

....

....

The Communication / Clarity Solution Path

What is your side of the story? What is theirs? Can you reach a compromise or figure out a new way to view the situation?

....
....
....
....
....
....
....
....
....
....

Is there another way to address it?

....
....
....
....
....
....
....

Part 3: Assess Challenges and Take Action

What is the outcome you want, and is it worth it?

....

....

....

....

....

....

Are you willing to stand your ground no matter what it might cost the relationship?

....

....

....

....

....

Imagine that the conversation goes well. What is a positive outcome that could result from it?

....

....

....

....

....

If the outcome means an improvement to the business or the behavior of a team member who needs to get back on track, or it takes an idea to the next step, it is worth it. Go into the meeting with an open mind and the aim of doing what is right for the business and look for areas where you can compromise. How you show up in these situations can create a positive or a negative perception of you.

Presenting to Others

Depending on the topic and the responsibility level of the audience in the room, presenting can be easy or high-pressure. The more senior the audience, the more preparation is needed to ensure that it goes well. Giving a presentation is a great way to get visibility in front of your leadership team, so it is worth doing. It gives them the opportunity to see you in action and observe how credible you are, the ownership you are taking, the quality of your decision-making, and your ability to lead the conversation.

REFLECTION QUESTION
What do you do to prepare for high-pressure presentations?

STEVE'S PREPARATION FOR THE CLIENT MEETING

We reviewed everything Steve wanted to say one last time and made sure that he had everything in order on the day of his presentation. I said, "You've done a great job with your preparation. What do you want your client to say to you after the meeting ends, Steve?" He pondered this for a moment and then said, "I want him to say it was a great presentation and he is looking forward to next quarter's review." "Wouldn't that be amazing!" I replied. "Go make it happen!"

He texted me later in the afternoon and said, "The client had very few questions compared to how many he normally asks, and he actually smiled!" I laughed when I saw that part. At the end of the text, Steve wrote, "He told me I did a great job! And 'See you next quarter!' Can you believe it? Such a different experience from last time! Thank you so much for your help!"

I texted him back, "That is amazing news! You should be so proud of yourself. You did all the preparation and the work and made it happen! I'm so happy for you! Congratulations!"

Steve's story is one of so many that I have had the pleasure of being a part of on this journey. It makes such a difference when you plan the story you want to tell and are strategic with the information you share. You can leverage any presentation to accomplish your visibility goal, whether it's one simple slide or a multi-page deck. Again, it is all about value and impact.

Tips to consider:

- Align on the purpose of the presentation and share the executive summary to give context.
- Demonstrate strategic leadership and confidently make an impact during the presentation.
- Lead the group and tell them what to pay attention to on the slides so they are listening to you and not reading them.
- Be concise and use facts and data to support your story and message. Less is more on the slides.

- Practice the presentation multiple times so you are prepared.
- Proactively address any potential objections in the presentation.

Final Thoughts

Clarity in communication makes all the difference in how a conversation goes and in getting agreement to move something forward. Confusion and misalignment cause the people in the room to doubt the information and impact the credibility of the presenter. Following the steps in this chapter will allow you to show up in the best way and accomplish your objectives. Take the time to be thoughtful and it will show!

Go to the resources page on the next page to access the action plan template and complete your plan.

Chapter Focus Areas and Reflection Questions

- Preparing for a conversation: *How do you prepare for a conversation?*
- Reframing conversations: *When you have conversations with stakeholders, do they show your value and the impact you are making?*
- Be strategic and succinct: *What can you do to get ready to share your thoughts in a meeting?*
- The Simple Communication Framework: *How will you ensure that everyone is on the same page at the beginning of your meetings?*
- Weaving in value and impact: *What opportunities do you have to say more about your skills, results, and what makes you unique in conversation?*
- Difficult conversations: *What has prevented you from having difficult conversations?*
- Presenting to others: *What do you do to prepare for high-pressure presentations?*

Part 3: Assess Challenges and Take Action

Resources:

This QR code will take you to the resources page where you will find your action plan template, podcasts, videos, and additional resources to support what you learned in this chapter.

Chapter 10
THE INFLUENCING / RELATIONSHIPS SOLUTION PATH

THIS CHAPTER INTRODUCES OPPORTUNITIES FOR you to build your influence and relationships to a greater extent.

Follow my client Sandy's journey through the influencing/relationships solution path to witness her process and open your awareness to more areas where you can increase your visibility.

SANDY'S STORY

Wait, what?

Sandy squirmed in her chair as she processed what her boss had just said to her. The rating he said she would receive caught her totally off guard. Just thirty minutes ago she had been smiling to herself as she walked down the hall to his office. She had filled her performance review with all the great things she had helped to deliver this year and given herself a high rating. She was shocked by what she heard, and she couldn't concentrate. *What is happening?*

No one should have this experience, but unfortunately it happens more often than you might expect, like when you're in a meeting and someone makes an offhanded comment without explanation or speaks over you and cuts you off. When this kind of situation occurs, it sends a silent message that what you have to say isn't valuable. So when it happens (not if, when), you owe it to yourself to explore what you need to do to address it. Leverage the ideas in this chapter to learn ways to handle this in the future.

Managing Up

A trust-based relationship with your manager will give you insights into the organization where you otherwise have limited access. You can learn about various conversations that have taken place, the politics of who is doing what, and upcoming changes that may impact you or your team. Each piece of information is like a puzzle piece that helps you fill in the picture of how things work and how to get things done. Having access to this information allows you to increase your influence and better understand how things work. It also helps you navigate upcoming challenges.

Ask where your manager could use your assistance. Understanding how to support them so they do well will help both you and your team. Your relationship with your manager is critical to achieving career success in an organization.

> **REFLECTION QUESTION**
>
> *What could you do to build a stronger relationship with your manager?*

> **SANDY'S MANAGER**
>
> Sandy thought she had a good working relationship with her boss and asked him for feedback in one-on-ones, but in his

rush to get to the next meeting, he would always just say "Things are fine." It was clear to her now that he didn't want to face her until he had to tell her otherwise in her review because he was a conflict avoider. Obviously, things weren't fine, and she was receiving all the feedback at once. Her self-confidence faltered with each new comment, and she felt disillusioned with her manager. *I thought I was adding so much value.*

She stopped listening and instead escaped by looking out the window. It had been a beautiful sunny day when she walked in, but now all she could see were gloomy clouds. This rating she was getting wasn't the worst, but it wasn't what she deserved. *Was all the work I delivered for nothing?*

She was so disappointed.

Later, we discussed the chart below in detail to help Sandy understand how to handle her relationships with her manager and other influencers in a more intentional way.

BENEFITS OF MANAGING UP

WHAT YOUR MANAGER / SENIOR LEADERS SHARE	WHAT YOU CAN LEARN
Gain Insights	
• Their extensive experience in and knowledge of the industry and organization can help you gain insight. • They can communicate a vision of where the company is going and how your role can play a part in the success of the goals of the company.	• You can also learn how they view their role, what they value, who they view as their allies in the organization, and what their own manager is telling them. • Understand their communication style so you take it into consideration when you meet and communicate with them.

Part 3: Assess Challenges and Take Action

Networking

- Having a conversation with a senior leader can help you build a network of contacts within the organization.
- This can be helpful in the future when you are looking for career opportunities, looking for advice, or seeking mentorship or referrals.

- You can learn who they meet with regularly and what they discuss during those meetings.
- Ask for recommendations of people they think you should meet within the company, or externally, so that you continue to gain new connections and perspectives.

Career Development

- Your leaders can help you gain a better understanding of the skills and knowledge you need to develop to advance your career within the organization.
- Your leaders can share feedback on your performance and ways to improve.

- You can learn about their career trajectory and let them know what you have an interest in doing next year or in a few years.
- Put your interests on their radar so that they will think of you if they hear of an opportunity that aligns with your career plan. Ask for feedback to ensure they are aligned with your plan.

Inspiration and Motivation

- They can inspire and motivate you with new ideas that help you approach your work in a more effective and innovative way.
- They can share their experiences and challenges in their career and help you understand how to navigate them.
- They can show you how they influence their own management team.

- You can learn how to coach team members by observing how they coach you.
- And you can learn how to solve problems and handle challenges with their support.

Visibility

- By meeting with a senior leader, you can raise your visibility within the organization. This can help to build your reputation and increase your chances of being considered for future career opportunities.
- If you feel like this could be a long relationship with them, you might consider asking them if they will be your mentor or sponsor.

- Meeting with your manager and other senior leaders is a great opportunity to share information about your team members.
- You can learn how your manager views your team and where the relationship may need to be supported.
- Think about how you can give exposure to your team in front of your manager or other influencers.

Figure 10.1: Benefits of Managing Up

Having a productive relationship with your boss helps you to learn their styles of management, leadership, and communication. Managing up is basically about building a positive and proactive relationship with those in leadership above you. You are there to assist your manager, deliver on expectations, and leverage their support when you need it.

MANAGING UP EXERCISE

What could you do to manage up more effectively?

....

....

....

....

....

....

How can you help your manager(s) achieve their goals and gain additional opportunities for visibility?

....

....

....

....

....

....

....

What strengths do you have that your manager doesn't, and how can you leverage those strengths to provide them with more support?

....

....

....

....

....

....

....

....

....

....

....

Meeting with Influencers

Meeting with influencers is necessary for building your brand and showing your value. Share your value and experience, what you can do, and what you want to do next with them. They are the people who can help you get things done and get a decision-maker to say yes when you need it. They can be leveraged to influence someone when the approaches you have taken don't work. Influencing is a two-way street. You influence others, and they influence you.

The Influencing / Relationships Solution Path

REFLECTION QUESTION
What would be different if you leveraged influencing and built more relationships?

SANDY BUILT INFLUENCER RELATIONSHIPS

Sandy's boss isn't the strongest leader. He wasn't helping her by holding back feedback she needed to hear. This is not uncommon. Leaders struggle to give feedback when it is constructive rather than purely positive, so they put it off. It would be great if Sandy's boss could help her to succeed where she needed it, but she realized she could leverage other relationships with influencers to do the same thing. Meeting with influencers gave her an opportunity to share her story, talk about the work being accomplished in her area, show her value, and increase her visibility.

At first, she was hesitant to meet some of these people. Her first words to me about it were, "I can't possibly meet with these people. I have no idea what to say, and why would they ever want to meet with me?"

So many of my clients over the years have said these exact words to me when we talk about the ways they can expand their network to meet the influencers in their organization. I said the same thing to my first mentor too. I couldn't imagine that people who were two levels or more above me would have time to meet with me, and if they said yes, what on earth would I say to them? Can you see where I wasn't valuing myself and had put them on a pedestal?

I walked Sandy through some information to help her with her conversations.

Best Practices to Follow with Influencers

Relationships with influencers get things moving faster in an organization and can help to propel your career. Don't wait until you need someone to meet with them. Your network should include people who have had the experience of working with you and understand where you bring value. It is important that you have the same knowledge of them as well. A single conversation could be valuable for your future. Here are some tips:

- When you meet someone new, focus on value first. They are a human being too. Be yourself, be authentic, and know that you are their equal.
- Find out what you can about them before the meeting. What have they done in their career? What is important to them? What do they care about? What do they do?
- Ask them about their career trajectory and how they progressed into their current role.
- Share about yourself, your background, what you are working on, and what makes you unique. Remember to focus on the value and impact you bring and ask questions to learn how you can support them in their role.
- If you want to continue the relationship with this person, ask if they would be open to meeting in the future to discuss (insert what you want to learn or share more details about).
- Ask them if there is anyone else you should meet with to keep building your network. If they have ideas, ask if it would be okay to use their name when introducing yourself to the new person. Thank them after you meet with the other person and share the outcome of the meeting with them.
- If you agreed to follow up with a contact, resource, or something else, send it over within a day. Thank them for their time and share what you enjoyed learning about them.

INFLUENCERS EXERCISE

Who do you need to build rapport with, in your function or in an adjacent group, that you may need help from in the next year?

....

....

....

....

Who are the people with influence in the organization who need to understand the value you bring?

....

....

....

....

....

Outside of your function, who else in the organization has influence and could help you in your career?

....

....

....

....

....

Influencing without Authority

Opportunities for you to be visible as a leader exist with a team that reports to you, but also when you are influencing others without holding any authority over them. Leading your own team is easier because they report to you. What happens, though, when you need to lead a project team or group of volunteers that doesn't report to you.

You have to use your influencing skills to inspire and motivate them.

> **REFLECTION QUESTION**
> *What if you thought of influence without authority as an opportunity to inspire or motivate someone?*

> **SANDY'S OPPORTUNITY TO INFLUENCE WITHOUT AUTHORITY**
>
> After Sandy's performance review, we talked about ways she could become better known in the organization. She said, "I could reconnect with the people I haven't met with recently, meet with more of the leaders in the company, and get more involved in the women's employee resource group."
>
> All these ideas were great, but she had an opportunity to take a leadership role with the resource group. This would show another side of her leadership, increase her visibility, and allow her to practice her influencing skills. She decided to contact the chairperson of the group and set up a conversation.

How can influencing without authority help your visibility?

- Building relationships is one of the most effective ways to exert influence without authority. Establish meaningful connections with your co-workers to foster trust and inspire them to help you achieve your goals.
- Position yourself as an expert. It makes influencing people to change their behavior easier. Thought leaders can drive meaningful change. To stand out as someone who inspires others and offers guidance, focus on your personal brand. Identify what makes you unique and build a brand that reflects your work and the value you bring to the table.
- Express your ideas in a way that makes people want to support you. One effective way to communicate with your team is through persuasive storytelling.
- When you are asked to lead without positional authority, embrace it! You're bound to encounter resistance from others. If there is pushback, take the time to learn where it is coming from and if you can address the issue. Otherwise, use it as an opportunity to explain your ideas in a more compelling way. View any type of opportunity like this as a chance to show your leadership and influence, be excited that you were asked (which means they see potential in you!), and know that you can ask for help if you need it. This is a chance to learn, grow and be visible.

Selling Isn't Just for Salespeople

To build visibility in an organization, put your selling and influencing skills to work. You can compile business cases to gain approval for projects, sell new ideas that will improve processes, build support for someone on your team to get a promotion, and strengthen your visibility at the same time. To gain approval for projects and access resources, I had to learn how to have bolder, more influential conversations and demonstrate managerial courage to challenge when necessary. All of

Part 3: Assess Challenges and Take Action

this increased my credibility, visibility, and confidence in leading those conversations in much bigger, even visionary ways.

REFLECTION QUESTION
Can you think of selling as a conversation first and influencing second?

SANDY'S INFLUENCING OPPORTUNITY

Sandy was given an opportunity to lead a new program that was starting soon. It would require her to identify the scope, put together the plan, and gain approval for funding. This was new for her, but she saw a chance to use the influencing skills she had been building. She would bring her ideas about expanding the messaging and create clarity around what needed to go in the plan. Although she had been having influential conversations, this would require a different kind of preparation.

PLANNING FOR AN INFLUENTIAL CONVERSATION EXERCISE

Spend time planning the conversation before it happens using the Influential Conversation Planner on the next page. Answer the questions in the table to the right to prepare.

The Influencing / Relationships Solution Path

INFLUENTIAL CONVERSATION PLANNER

What outcome do you want from the meeting?	
What is important to and valued by the person you are meeting? (For example, priorities, goals, objectives, etc.)	
Does the story you are telling say what they need to hear so you can get to an easy yes?	
Have you included costs, benefits, data, and options for them to review?	
What do you want them to provide for you? (A review? Feedback? Their approval?)	
What did you learn that you want to include in or consider when planning your next conversation?	

The people who prepare for big conversations with intention are able to demonstrate success and proactively address questions in advance. You may need to garner support from others beforehand to get feedback and ensure that you have included everything you need in your plan.

Networking

Are you someone who avoids networking events when you have to attend alone? That was definitely me, and my self-critic was the loudest voice in the room, though I was the only one to hear her. Again, understand that your fear in these moments drives the inner critic to get even louder. Take a breath and meet with one person at a time. Have some questions prepared in advance. You will find that things will be much more enjoyable.

REFLECTION QUESTION

What if one person you meet could make a big impact for you simply through having a conversation with them?

SANDY FOCUSED ON NETWORKING

Sandy had done many things to build her personal brand and be viewed as a leader. She recognized that she also needed to build her network, both internally and externally.

Having a strong external network is an important asset to have at all times. She reconnected with people in her network and attended a few networking sessions with a local women's organization.

The Influencing / Relationships Solution Path

Imagine if you spoke with one person each week. Within a year you would have connected with fifty-two people who now have updated BASE files about you while you have theirs too. Connections are beneficial, so do more networking. It works.

Note: If you are just getting started in your career, there are hundreds of ideas for how to influence, build relationships, network, and so much more in Chapter 6 of *The Visibility Factor*. The ideas are divided by level of experience. If you want more ideas, or details on any of the ways to be more visible, it is a great resource! Additionally, I have three podcasts for you to listen to on networking that include questions to use, how to prepare, and an interview with a master networker! There is a QR code at the end of this chapter that will take you to all the resources.

The goal is to meet new people. You don't have to meet everyone in the room, but networking events are a good opportunity to meet at least five to ten new people. Always come from a place of value and use follow-up questions to learn more about your new acquaintances. You can leverage them for help, or they may need yours.

Are You Networking to Find a New Role?

Being visible and networking with others who can help you is critical when you need to find a new role. Some things to keep in mind when networking for a new role that many people aren't aware of (but now *you* are):

- Always assume people want to help you; 70 to 80 percent of new roles are found through networking.
- List contacts who could help you and connect with them. (Don't discount anyone—remember, there are only six degrees of separation between you and the people you want to meet.)

- Keeping your personal brand in mind, prepare your elevator pitch (remember the template that Mary from finance used in Chapter 9), along with examples, stories, and other information to share during networking sessions.
- During networking conversations, ask who else you should meet with and if the person you are speaking with would be willing to make the connection.
- Set up informational interviews with people who have similar roles and learn what happens in their day.
- Expect the best out of conversations. Even if you are happy in your company, you should always be networking.

Final Thoughts

Starting with value for the other person is always the best first step. Taking conversations to a deeper level and showing the value you bring is where the big impact lies. Leveraging the tools in this path will help you prepare and plan for these conversations and to maintain relationships. Take the time to build and influence relationships in an organization to get the work done and show your value and impact.

Go to the resources section on the next page to access the action plan template and complete your plan.

Chapter Focus Areas and Reflection Questions:

- Managing up: *What could you do to build a stronger relationship with your manager?*
- Meeting with influencers: *What would be different if you leveraged influencing and built more relationships?*
- Influence without authority: *What if you thought of influence without authority as an opportunity to inspire or motivate someone?*
- Selling isn't only for salespeople: *Can you think of selling as a conversation first and influencing second?*

- Networking: *What if one person you meet could make a big impact for you simply through having a conversation with them?*

Resources

Use this QR code to take you to the resources page. It includes your action plan template, podcasts, videos, and additional resources to support what you learned in this chapter.

Chapter 11
THE LEADING / BEING STRATEGIC SOLUTION PATH

IN THIS CHAPTER, YOU WILL learn how leading and being strategic have a big impact on your visibility. The way you show up as a leader of a team, program, or big project matters. What you do and say tells a story about your ability to do more at your current level and whether you are ready to move on to the next.

Follow Lisa's story and how she navigated this path to increase her visibility at her company.

> **LISA'S CLIENT STORY**
>
> "I have listened to the feedback and done what was asked, but my management still doesn't think I am ready to be a director. I want to present myself in a way that shows them I am ready."

Lisa shared this comment at our first session. She spoke quickly and in a tone of frustration. I could tell she had been trying to break through this issue for a while and couldn't figure out how to do anything different. I asked her to share what feedback she had received, and she rolled her eyes as she said, "They told me that I just wasn't ready yet!" Vague feedback is hard to act on. I could understand why it would frustrate her. We talked about her visibility and although she had taken a few opportunities to try new things, she admitted that she could do more.

Being Visible As a Leader

You read some of the ways that visibility was defined in Chapter 4. You now understand what it means and why it is important to career success. However, you need to be strategic about your visibility. Don't try to do everything; rather, choose to take the actions that will move the needle the most.

It is important to stay true to yourself. Choose the opportunities that work best for you and take actions that are authentic to you. The VALUE Framework I introduced in Chapter 6 is built for the sole purpose of helping you to be intentional with your visibility. I don't want you to create extra work for yourself. Leverage what you are already doing to become more visible. Remember the study in Chapter 4 that showed that 73 percent of promotions are given to leaders when they are in front of decision-makers? Your main goal on this path is to get in front of decision-makers. They need to know you, like you, and trust that you can do the job you have, and you need to show them that you are ready for future opportunities.

> **REFLECTION QUESTION**
> *Am I doing enough to be visible
> to decision-makers?*

LISA'S VISIBILITY PLAN

Lisa had great visibility opportunities outside of her company as a speaker representing the company at conferences. It was challenging for her to replicate the same level of visibility internally. She was viewed as a subject matter expert, and it served her well for a long time, but she had to step out of that role to be viewed as a director. It was important to figure out the right path for Lisa to follow.

I took her through an exercise similar to the one you are about to do: We reviewed what she had been doing already, other opportunities she had for visibility, and other areas of focus she hadn't yet considered, and prioritized what would be most beneficial given her time investment. We built her visibility plan and focused on the challenges of increasing her visibility, developing her team to lead on their own, and helping to demonstrate that she was ready to be a director.

I have similar conversations with all of my clients to learn what they can take advantage of in their day. We explore what they have been doing, other current opportunities, and additional areas of future potential and prioritize those actions with the most benefit to provide a structure to follow. We start with exploring the answers to the questions below. This may be the first time they are venturing out of their comfort zone to consider additional visibility, and the exercises allow them to start considering new possibilities. Let's go through these questions for you now.

EXPLORE VISIBILITY OPPORTUNITIES EXERCISE

What have you done to be visible?

....

....

Part 3: Assess Challenges and Take Action

What other current opportunities do you have?

What additional opportunities could you leverage in the future?

Identify the opportunities that will give you the biggest return on your time investment.

Remote Leadership

Though many companies are pushing for a return to the office now, remote leadership is still a needed skill. You can benefit from leading teams local to you but also lead people in multiple locations globally. Plenty of opportunities exist to leverage technology to have good conversations. I always advocate for you to meet your team members in person at least once to establish the connection. After that, you need to ensure that you stay consistently connected, with intention. Your team needs to believe that you are there to support them whether you see them every day or not.

HOW LISA HANDLES REMOTE VISIBILITY

Lisa operates from a remote location 80 to 90 percent of the time. She makes the effort to be at the headquarters location and visit other locations at least once a month. Nothing can replace face time, so she needs to be creative to stay in front of decision-makers. She is very intentional about getting on people's calendars for one-on-ones and makes good use of her in-person time by having meetings set up in advance, including lunches and dinners when possible.

I have another client who had team members located all across the United States. They came together during the pandemic to create one of the strongest teams I have seen while all fully remote. Listen to Episode 12 of *The Visibility Factor* podcast with my client, Jen Fox, (I have included a QR code that links to it and other resources at the end of this chapter) to hear how she built a team that is engaged, connected, and making an impact. She has now done the same with a new team. It is possible when you put intention behind it!

REMOTE TEAM MEMBERS EXERCISE

How can you stay more connected to your remote team members or to other leaders that work remotely from you? What did you learn about this from the podcast? What are some of your own ideas?

1. _____

   _____

   _____

2. ....

....

....

3. ....

....

....

What if you are the employee and searching for ways to be more visible? It is absolutely possible to be visible when working remotely, but you need to be intentional about it. Speaking up on remote calls isn't always easy, but you can find ways to do it. Put yourself on the agenda, talk to the meeting leader beforehand and state that you have something to discuss, or advocate for meetings that are more inclusive of everyone's voice, whether they are in the room or not.

You can also take advantage of some of the ideas I share in Chapter 10 of *The Visibility Factor*. I included the top challenges of working remotely and solutions for each one. You can also listen to Episode 72 of *The Visibility Factor* podcast (again, see the end of this chapter for the QR code that will take you to the resources page), which is all about ideas for remote leadership and what I did when I had team members around the globe.

Mindset Shift

Stepping up into higher levels of leadership and strategy requires reflection on your readiness, intention, and motivation. Are you ready to be uncomfortable but excited about the opportunities that come next? Having a strong growth mindset allows you to navigate whatever comes your way, whether things are going well or you are being challenged.

You can achieve what you want when you believe in yourself and what you are doing. The first step to taking bigger actions is having a corresponding vision of yourself.

I love to help people discover new things about themselves and possibilities for what they can accomplish. In Chapter 3, you focused on what you want for your future and created a future state vision. Based on what you want, you may have to play much bigger than you are today.

REFLECTION QUESTION
Who do you need to be to achieve your future?

LISA'S MINDSET SHIFT

Now that I understood Lisa's frustrations and what she had done to gain visibility so far, it was time to focus on her mindset. I asked her to define how she wanted to be seen as a leader. She responded, "A leader who doesn't ask for permission, but takes ownership of the work and the team and has a strong influence on the organization."

Change only happens when someone is open to seeing themselves in a new way and getting out of their comfort zone. Notice that Lisa was focused on who she "needed to be" to create the outcome of being seen differently. She had to shift her mindset first and believe she could be this type of leader in order to take new actions. Lisa needed to start being this new person so she could step into a higher level of leadership, visibility, and confidence—the transformation that others would see in her.

The Leading / Being Strategic Solution Path

MINDSET SHIFT EXERCISE

How do you want to be seen as a leader?

....

....

....

....

....

....

Who do you "need to be" now to become the leader you just described?

....

....

....

....

....

....

Leading with Visibility

Note: You might be tempted to skip this section if you don't have a team right now. I invite you to read through it anyway. Are there opportunities to develop others or ask for support? You can lead with visibility at any level.

Taking on a leadership role means leading a team, project, program, or organization. It means that you switch from being the doer to the person who leads the doers. Since you are no longer the one doing the work, a shift in mindset is required. This transition is one of the most challenging for leaders to navigate. You are known for getting work done and then, all of a sudden, the thing that you are known for isn't what you are supposed to do anymore. This becomes an issue for leaders who don't trust themselves to lead and revert to being doers again. They worry about how they are perceived and don't want anything to fall through the cracks, so they give their team the answers instead of coaching them and may do their team's work for them to ensure that due dates are met. They have no idea how apparent it is to others that they are doing the work instead of leading the team.

> **REFLECTION QUESTION**
> *Are you leading with visibility and helping others to do the same?*

LISA'S LEADERSHIP SHIFT

Coaching her team to own their work became Lisa's primary focus. We talked about how to motivate her team and help them focus on what they needed to learn for future opportunities. They needed to be able to manage the work without her, so instead of giving her team the answers, she coached them instead. She spent time helping them learn how to solve problems. She showed she trusted them by delegating to them, sending them to meetings in her place, and giving them ownership of their projects. She became an escalation point instead of a subject matter expert who was always answering questions.

The Leading / Being Strategic Solution Path

Here is why embracing leadership is so important. You can't blame your team for their ineffectiveness, although many leaders will try. It is your responsibility to help them and provide guidance in a way that speaks to their style, not yours. Each employee can be at a different level and need different things from you. Understand what motivates them, and how to support them both individually and as a group. Giving the hard feedback and redirecting their actions so that they show up appropriately is absolutely necessary. If they aren't the right fit, you may have to make the difficult decision to let them go.

It is your role to ensure that you have the best team doing the work. You may have to make a tough call to fire someone or give them a lower rating if they aren't performing. Leading isn't easy, and it requires many moments of courage to challenge others, disagree, and stand up for your team. If you don't deal with difficult situations, it will create doubt in others' minds about your ability to lead that may impact your future career plans. If you aren't able to lead at the level where you are now, the next level isn't up for discussion until you do.

LEADERSHIP CHECK-IN EXERCISE

On a scale of 1–10 (10 being the highest), how would you rate yourself on your ability to let your team (direct reports or any other people you lead) do the work without giving them all the answers? Circle your answer below?

1   2   3   4   5   6   7   8   9   10

What percentage of your time each week is spent in the following areas? Write your percentages below.

Coaching: _____   **Telling:** _____   **Listening:** _____

Part 3: Assess Challenges and Take Action

On a scale of 1–10 (10 being the highest), how would your management rate you on how well you develop your team? Circle your answer below.

    1   2   3   4   5   6   7   8   9   10

Do you have any opportunities to demonstrate your leadership in a bigger way?

....

....

....

....

....

....

....

....

....

....

....

....

....

....

Being Liked vs. Being Respected

Leaders who worry about upsetting someone if they make the wrong decision, or let things slide to avoid confrontation, care more about being liked than being respected. Every one of my clients has heard me say that it is more important to be respected than liked. Leaders who want to be liked worry excessively about how they are perceived. They are afraid to stand out or challenge others when necessary. Their fear will get in the way and cause them to take the easy way out instead of doing what is right. Respected leaders do what is right for the company, their department, and their team. Their decisions aren't always the most popular, but they will be respected for making the difficult choice when needed.

REFLECTION QUESTION
Are you viewed as a leader who is liked or a leader who is respected?

LISA'S OPPORTUNITY TO GAIN RESPECT

When organizational changes were occurring in the company, Lisa's manager shared that another team would be moving into their organization. He inferred that the leader of the new group would report to him. She challenged his idea and said, "I would be interested in taking on the team and integrating everyone together under me. This group will need more support to understand what we do, and I can help them all come together." This was an opportunity to help her leader focus on what he needed to do and demonstrate that she was ready to take on more. Her logic was sound and showed that she was focused on what was best for the team and the organization. He agreed with her, and she took over the new group.

Part 3: Assess Challenges and Take Action

The table below shows the differences between leaders who are liked and leaders who are respected.

LEADERS WHO ARE RESPECTED	SITUATIONS	LEADERS WHO ARE LIKED
Deliver hard feedback	**FEEDBACK**	Avoid giving feedback
Challenge the status quo in order to improve	**COMPANY PROBLEMS**	Accept the current state
Are open to change	**ORGANIZATIONAL CHANGES**	Struggle with change
Don't ask for permission	**TAKES INITIATIVE**	Hesitate without gathering opinions from others or permission from the manager
Have the courage to terminate someone	**PERFORMANCE MANAGEMENT**	Take no action to address issues
Make the hard choices	**DECISION-MAKING**	Avoid the hard choices
Hold people accountable for doing their work	**PERFORMANCE ISSUES**	Don't say or do anything when due dates are missed by a team member
Stay composed during times of high stress	**HIGH-STRESS SITUATIONS**	Show stress and an inability to manage issues

Figure 11.1: Leaders Who Are Respected vs. Leaders Who Are Liked

BEING LIKED VS. BEING RESPECTED EXERCISE

Based on the list of characteristics for each type, do you see an area where you may be too focused on being liked?

....

....

....

....

....

....

....

....

....

....

....

....

Strategic Visibility

As you move into higher leadership roles, you will be expected to think and act strategically. If you haven't done it before, it isn't easy to flip a switch and magically become a strategic thinker. It would be great if it worked that way, but it doesn't, especially if your brain has been focused on execution for years. It is easier to be busy and focus on doing than plan a strategy, build your first business case, create a proposal, or prepare to present an idea. If your intention is to climb to a higher level, it is necessary to build your strategic skills and give yourself enough time to think and plan.

> **REFLECTION QUESTION**
> *Are you giving yourself adequate time
> each week to think and plan?*

LISA'S STRATEGY MOMENTS

Lisa focused her time on executing her visibility plan consistently and intentionally to show her leadership that she was ready. She had conversations with executive leadership about her ideas and the work she was doing with her team and communicated that a promotion was her goal. She was thoughtful, strategic, and leveraged all of her available opportunities. Her team stepped up and owned their work. She went from being told that she "wasn't ready" for the next step to being promoted to a director. The decision became an easy one for the leadership team to make because she had proven she was ready!

What Is Strategy?

The definition of strategy is "a careful plan or method."[22] That sounds so simple, doesn't it? Let's focus on strategy in terms of visibility, though. Each of the solution paths has various strategies to leverage, but are you being strategic with your visibility opportunities?

That starts with intention, consistency, and being in front of decision-makers. Remember when you filled out the VALUE Framework the first time? Did you identify opportunities to be more visible that you could take advantage of? Keep doing it. You are doing so much more than the many leaders who never even consider their visibility.

I can't resist an opportunity to share ideas, so here are a few to consider if you want to demonstrate leadership in a more strategic way:

- Sell an idea
- Build a business case
- Lead a project
- Lead a team
- Lead an employee resource group
- Speak externally
- Volunteer for a special project
- Ask to be included in a company or external leadership program
- Mentor junior members of the company
- Join an industry association or affinity group

Reading through this list, did you identify any ideas that are new to you?

Strategic Visibility Opportunity Exercise

Choose one of the ideas from above or use your own and explore what it could do for you and your visibility. Capture details and what your next action step would be to try it out.

....

....

....

....

....

....

Part 3: Assess Challenges and Take Action

Any one of the ideas I listed will increase your visibility if you want; you simply need to put a plan in place that works for you and then take action. You can do this. I did it and my clients have done it. You might be saying to yourself, *Well, they had you to help them.* Yes, they did. You have this workbook, though. I have given you all the tools to plan and be strategic with your opportunities. Don't overthink it, just act. Use the VALUE Framework to stay intentional and consistent each week.

Final Thoughts

Do you view leading and strategy in a different way now? Ask for help from peers, your manager, a mentor, or a coach. One of my favorite things to do is help someone identify ways to be more strategic with their visibility. What you are doing right now is building awareness, and that will become easier for you once you really focus on it. When you give yourself the time and space to plan, you will execute in a more thoughtful way and others will be able to see you as the leader who is ready for the next step. It's time for you to get started with your focus areas to build your action plan!

Go to the resources section on the next page to access the action plan template and complete your plan.

Chapter Focus Areas and Reflection Questions

- Being visible as a leader: *Am I doing enough to be visible to decision-makers?*
- Mindset shift: *Who do you need to be to achieve your future?*
- Leading with visibility: *Are you leading with visibility and helping others to do the same?*
- Being liked vs. being respected: *Are you viewed as a leader who is liked or respected?*
- Strategic visibility: *Are you giving yourself adequate time each week to think and plan?*

Part 3: Assess Challenges and Take Action

Resources

This QR code will take you to the resources page, which includes your action plan template, podcasts, videos, and additional resources to support what you learned in this chapter.

Chapter 12
THE JOURNEY CONTINUES

"Life Moves Pretty Fast. If you don't stop and look around once in a while, you could miss it."

Ferris Bueller, played by Matthew Broderick, breaks the fourth wall to share this famous line directly with the audience in the mid-1980s movie *Ferris Bueller's Day Off*.[23] In case you haven't seen it, at the beginning of the movie Ferris is still in bed but decides he wants to skip high school that day. (We can all relate to wanting to take a day or two off from high school, right?) He convinces his parents that he is too ill to go to school and needs to stay home, but his real plan is to explore downtown Chicago with his friends. Ferris is charismatic, bold, unafraid to take risks, and trying to see what he can get away with for the day. His hidden agenda, though, is to show his uptight, skeptical friend Cameron, played by Alan Ruck, that life is passing him by and if he would just stop and look around, he would see that it can be pretty wonderful.

I love this quote because it is a good reminder to us all, including leaders, to slow down and look around. Finding the time to gain new perspective, reflect, and plan is not a high priority for most leaders. Our culture is focused on being busy and doing the low-value things that we can cross off our lists. If you want to achieve career success, though, you need to focus on high-value work and let go of anything else. Be strategic and leverage the high-value work to its full potential for your and your team's visibility.

Be the Student

The title of Chapter 1 in *The Visibility Factor* is "When the Student is Ready, the Teacher Appears." That opening chapter focuses on the conversations I had with my personal and business mentors regarding my lack of visibility. The first conversation with my personal mentor was difficult, and although the teaching moment was necessary, I can't say I was at all ready for it!

The second conversation with my business mentor was a completely different experience. She helped me learn that it was important to find the time to focus on my visibility and that I wasn't utilizing the time I had effectively. I had a responsibility to show up for myself and my team in a bigger way. She helped me understand what was needed, but it was up to me to figure out how to make it happen and design each day with intention, including plans I would execute to show my value. It was a big wake-up call.

When you have a problem, you need people you can trust to help you through it and tell you the truth. You may be surprised at who the teacher turns out to be, and the timing may be unexpected. On the surface, Ferris Bueller would never be viewed as a teacher by most people, especially his school principal (inside joke for those who have seen the movie)! However, if you view the movie through the lens of Ferris as teacher or mentor, you will see that he spent the entire day pushing the boundaries in everything they did to show Cameron that he could have fun, try new things, and enjoy life.

HEATHER'S STORY

A new client named Heather was a few months into her transition to a new company when she asked me to coach her!

I found her to be smart, capable, and excited for this new role. I learned during our first call that she had recently left a toxic workplace with managers who had disrespected and dismissed her, leading her to believe that she wasn't good enough. She wanted a clean start in her new company and to let go of the past. However, a few months into her transition, she continued to show signs that her decision-making and confidence were colored by the past.

As a coach, you have to keep digging to understand what is happening below the surface. Heather told me about how her manager had been supporting her during the first few months of the transition. Based on what she shared, I could tell he was still too involved. He had been making what should have been her decisions, taking meetings with her clients, and meeting with her team. She was frustrated by what was happening but didn't think about why. This was a blind spot for her until we talked about it. "There are two reasons why this might be happening," I told her. "The first is that he doesn't recognize he is overstepping at this point, and the second is that you might unintentionally be sending the message that you still need his help. Which do you think it is?"

Her facial expression showed her realization when she heard me say the options. She said, "It is definitely number two." This was a wake-up call for Heather. She was "playing not to lose" and asking for permission to avoid mistakes. She had been seeking permission for so long that it had become a habit. Working for toxic leaders leaves internal wounds that aren't always obvious, but now she saw them clearly and understood what was holding her back from being the leader she wanted to be.

We put a plan in place to change how she showed up with her manager, reframed her language to demonstrate that she was an equal, and helped her trust herself to lead conversations and deliver her work without any external validation.

> The changes have started to pay off. Recently, Heather left me a message saying, "Major shifts happened this week! My manager told me he had complete confidence in my ability to lead my team and process. I am acting like an equal to my manager and others in the company. I am not asking for permission anymore and I trust that what I am doing is right. I recently added another team under me, and I am confidently taking a proactive approach to meeting with my new clients and setting my teams up for success!"

Heather's story highlights the multiple challenges that can impact a leader. Did you recognize some of her challenges based on the work you completed in this workbook? You will be able to identify these types of situations for yourself and your team now. Helping team members navigate their transitions and challenges is part of a leader's role. Use what you have learned to help identify what could be happening for them.

I am so grateful to do the work I do. I get to be the teacher I always wanted to be (no chalkboards and chalk, but sometimes whiteboards and markers!) and help people see new possibilities for their identities, careers, and lives. I have put my heart and soul into helping leaders recognize their value and believe in themselves. It took me a long time to see my own value, and I don't want anyone else to have to wait, especially you! Now that you have reached the end of this workbook, what is possible for you? You can make a bigger impact in your career and your life, starting today. Why wait?

Never Give Up

Creating this workbook has been such a joy for me. It has given me the opportunity to coach and support you. The journey you have taken so far may have been easy to manage in some places and more difficult in others; since my role as a coach is to push you out of your comfort zone, I hope you worked through those difficult parts and tried new things. Did you surprise yourself? Are you proud of what you have accomplished?

A journey implies going from one place to another, it generally takes a long time, and it isn't always easy. In the words of Theodore Roosevelt, "Nothing in the world is worth having or worth doing unless it means effort, pain, difficulty…."[24] To improve requires perseverance and the will to overcome some adversity.

My goal with this workbook is to create a journey that challenges you and helps you see yourself in a new way. Every journey involves some adversity, but I want to lessen it for you where I can. I have shared what worked for me and what didn't. You have seen what I share with clients to help them move through their challenges and get to the other side where they are confident, influential, and making a difference. I want that for you too! Are you willing to let go of the side of the pool and swim into the deep end to try new things?

It is really tempting to stop trying to be seen and heard when things get hard. You may have tried different actions and conversations but found that nothing has worked quite yet. Promise me you won't give up. Will you push through any adversity that you encounter along the way? You can do this, and you have a responsibility to do it for yourself and your team if you have one.

> Remember Amelia from Chapter 2? She was the client who wanted to be viewed as a leader, but her management didn't believe she was ready. Amelia had some major perception challenges to overcome. In an email she sent me about a month after our last session, she shared the following:

> "I accepted a global role in a different function that is considered one of the highest-growth areas of the company. There are enormous opportunities for visibility, and the choice of roles after this position is practically limitless. Thank you for your coaching. I'm happy to finally be able to share the tangible success we were working toward."

What I love about Amelia's story is that she stayed focused on her goal. She wanted a new role and for people to see her as a leader. She never gave up on herself and we crafted the story she shared with each person so they could recognize the value she brings. We found ways to weave her passions into her conversations to build stronger relationships and grow her confidence.

Brave, bold leaders stand out. When you show up consistently, people will notice you. An amazing postscript to this story is that Amelia's manager told her she was making an exceptional impact in her new role during her performance review! This is what self-belief, confidence, and showing your value can do for you! I hope Amelia's story will inspire you. You don't need to be overlooked and unknown anymore.

What Comes Next?

Although this is the end of the workbook, the journey doesn't end here; it is only the beginning. I bet you are saying to yourself, *Wait, there's more?* You have been a great student, and you know more than most now. It's time for you to keep doing what works, teach others, and spread the insights you have learned to inspire others to show their value too. The truth is that you will continue to take on different roles and have new experiences that require you to show up in bigger ways. Visibility doesn't lessen when you take on more responsibilities; it needs to grow. That's why this is a journey to visibility.

The Journey Continues

Here are some tips for continuing the journey.

- Leverage the VALUE Framework to ensure that you are intentional and consistent with your visibility. Show your value and make an impact.
- Review the workbook when a situation comes up and you aren't sure what to do. Everything will be here for you to leverage as you navigate whatever changes arise and to provide support when you need it.
- Remember that positioning messages in such a way that people can hear you and envision you in future roles makes all the difference to your achievement of success.
- You understand yourself after completing the Visibility and Career Growth Framework. You appreciate your value and what you have learned and can leverage them in the future. Review the Visibility and Career Growth Framework each year to see how you have developed, where you are at that time, and where you want to go next.
- Meet people and let them in so they can help build awareness of what you have to offer—and so you can understand more about them too.
- Remember, when the student is ready, the teacher appears. Keep your workbook handy and you can use the templates, examples, and ideas when you need them!

Jen has been on her own journey to visibility. She read my book and has been a big supporter of mine. She did a test drive of the materials when I was finalizing this workbook and shared this feedback with me:

"I'm using [the VALUE Framework] weekly, on certain days. I had an aha moment reflecting on past work experiences and

> came to realize why my first instinct is to want to "pave my own way" before engaging my leaders. Great realizations here, and now that I'm aware I can recalibrate. I also found fantastic value in creating my 'sales pitch' and even sent out a survey to about fifteen people for feedback. I haven't read responses yet, so I'm looking forward to seeing what people said and maybe recalibrating even more. I enjoyed this and my immediate feedback is that THIS WORK IS ACTIONABLE! I'd love to see this used in a series of working sessions, maybe even in a mentor circle setting. This is really practical material that provides so much value/visibility."

I have delivered everything I promised to support you and your success on this journey to greater visibility. The ability to show your value and talk about your results will support you in so many situations, and there is no need to hold yourself back anymore. You don't have to figure everything out. All the ideas and solutions are right here for you. The "map" to follow is in your hands, along with the tools and resources to show your value, maximize your visibility, and confidently position yourself for the opportunities you want in your career!

Endings can be hard, but this is an exciting time for you. It's time for you to start taking bigger actions to achieve your future vision. Trust yourself, focus on your value, and make those future possibilities a reality! I believe in you and will be cheering for you every step of the way! You can do it!

Actions

Here are some ways to tap into my support and become a part of my community. Join us!

The Journey Continues

- Join the Be Bold, Be Visible, Be the Leader You Were Meant to Be Facebook group to connect with other readers of this workbook.[25]
- To hear about my latest programs and get new resources, sign up for my weekly newsletter that goes out each Saturday! https://susanmbarber.com
- Share on social media when you finish the workbook and tag your post with #yourjourneytovisibility. Be sure to tag me, too, so I can cheer you on!
- I would be so grateful if you would leave a review of the workbook on the site that you purchased it from. Include what made a difference for you and it will inspire someone else. (If you read *The Visibility Factor*, you can leave a review for the book too! I don't want the first child [book] to think I am favoring the second! LOL!) Thank you!
- If your company would benefit from having me come in and talk about visibility or take a group through the workbook process, please contact me! I would love to spread the message of visibility to as many leaders as possible. Thank you in advance! Contact me via email, or on my website.
- Share your successes with me! Send an email to hello@susanmbarber.com and share how things are going for you. Put "I am showing my VALUE!" in the subject line and share the details, and I will send you a personal note of congratulations. I can't wait to find out what you accomplished with your visibility!

Appendix

This appendix contains the following templates for you to use for your weekly VALUE plan and your Visibility Action plan:

- The VALUE Framework Plan
- The 90-Day Visibility Action Plan

Your Journey to Visibility Workbook **VALUE** Framework Plan: Week of ....

FRAMEWORK DEFINITION	WEEKLY ACTION PLAN
V - VISIBILITY — Identify new Visibility opportunities.	
What opportunities can I leverage for visibility this week?	
A - AMPLIFY — Amplify your influence, your team, your voice, and your accomplishments.	
Who needs to know me or hear about current work, past work team updates, or new ideas?	
L - LANGUAGE — Use strategic Language that tells the story and helps you lead conversations.	
What conversations can I lead with influence, impact, and strategic language this week?	
U - UNIQUE — To help you stand out, Leverage what makes you Unique and what you are known for.	
What can I do to increase my personal brand, gain new experiences, and leverage my strengths this week?	
E - EVALUATE — Evaluate your wins, value, impact, and missed opportunities.	
How did I add value this week? Did I achieve my VALUE plan? What did I learn to apply to my plan for next week?	

Appendix

90-Day Visibility Action Plan

WHAT YOU SAY AND DO MATTERS
SHOW YOUR VALUE AND MAKE AN IMPACT

Name: _____ Dates: _____

Write Your Leadership Vision Statement Below: (I am a leader who...)

Top 3 Goals/Outcomes	Key Actions to Achieve Results

Overall 90-Day Results

www.susanmbarber.com | Copyright 2025 Susan M Barber Coaching & Consulting, LLC

Your Journey to Visibility Workbook

Support & Resources Needed

Coaching Needs/Resources (e.g., feedback on communication style, developing influence, strategic thinking, podcasts, articles, books, training programs, internal mentors))

End of 90-Day Reflection

What worked well?

What feedback did you receive?

Do you feel different? Have you noticed a difference in how others behave around you?

What needs to change for the next 90 days?

Note

Regularly review and update this plan. It's a living document to guide your visibility and leadership development. Celebrate small wins and adjust as needed

Acknowledgments

THIS WORKBOOK WOULDN'T EXIST WITHOUT all of my clients and workshop attendees. They have given me so many opportunities to help them learn how to be visible. The conversations, presentations, workshops, and coaching sessions have all challenged me to create more ways to learn about visibility and share them with you. Special thanks to the clients who allowed me to share their stories in this workbook. Visibility and showing your value are now a part of who you are, and I am so honored to have been a part of your journey!

Thank you to AJ Harper, Laura Stone, the Top Three Book Workshop group and the Madeline Island editing retreat group, who helped me get this workbook off the ground! "Second books are hard to write," a wise person said to me. They were right, and these groups supported me and helped me believe it was possible!

To my Amplify You cohort group, early testers of my ideas and frameworks, you spent a year learning and growing! I'm so proud of you and grateful to you for sharing all your feedback. Special thanks to the workbook test-drive group, whose honesty led me to a new approach and allowed this workbook to become the final version that you hold in your hands now. I appreciate all of you for your time and willingness to help me see a better way!

Thank you to my family, Mike, Manda, Kelly, and Jack, who were so incredibly understanding when I had deadlines to meet and supported me through it all!

Thank you to all my friends and family who have also been so supportive of me and always ask how things are going with my book!

Thank you to Lori Young and her team, who consistently help me be visible in the world!

Thank you to Choi Messer, my designer; Zoë Bird, my copy editor; and KellyAnn Bessa, my proofreader, for continuing to be there to "catch" me when we go on these book journeys together! You are all incredibly talented and I am so grateful for all of you!

About the Author

SUSAN M BARBER, AUTHOR, PODCAST host, and former Fortune 500 IT director turned certified executive coach, specializes in transforming quiet, under-the-radar high achievers into visible, confident, influential leaders. She brings strong business and IT knowledge to her coaching from twenty-five-plus years of leadership experience at Kraft Heinz. Susan is the author of *The Visibility Factor* and the *Your Journey to Visibility Workbook* and the host of *The Visibility Factor* podcast. Her mission is to spread her visibility message and help leaders learn how to show their value and be seen for their true talent.

Endnotes

Introduction

[1] Brené Brown, *Dare to Lead: Brave Work. Tough Conversations. Whole Hearts* (Random House, 2018).

Chapter 1

[2] *The Proposal*, directed by Anne Fletcher (Walt Disney Studios, 2009).

Chapter 3

[3] Maya Angelou quote, Goodreads.com, https://www.goodreads.com/quotes/7273813-do-the-best-you-can-until-you-know-better-then (last accessed July 23, 2025)

[4] "The Evolution of Careers Over the Last 50 Years," https://saragossa.co.uk/the-evolution-of-careers-over-the-last-50-years, (last accessed August 6, 2025).

[5] Visit the Be Bold, Be Visible, Be the Leader You Are Meant to Be Facebook community: https://www.facebook.com/groups/265115150545457.

Chapter 4

[6] Merriam-Webster.com, definition of "visibility," https://www.merriam-webster.com/dictionary/visibility (last accessed July 23, 2025).

[7] Harvey Coleman, *Empowering Yourself: The Organizational Game Revealed* (AuthorHouse, revised edition, 2010).

[8] Marian N. Ruderman and Patricia J. Ohlott, "The Realities of Management Promotion," Center for Creative Leadership, 1994, https://www.ccl.org/wp-content/uploads/2015/04/ RealitiesMgtPromotion.pdf (last accessed July 23, 2025).

[9] Byron Katie and Stephen Mitchell, *Loving What Is: Four Questions That Can Change Your Life* (Harmony Books, 2003).

[10] Brad Yates website: https://www.tapwithbrad.com/faq-s (last accessed July 23, 2025).

[11] KPMG International, "KPMG Women's Leadership Study: Moving Women Forward into Leadership Roles," KPMG.com, 2015, https://assets.kpmg.com/content/dam/kpmg/ph/pdf/ThoughtLeadershipPublications/KPMGWomensLeadershipStudy.pdf (last accessed July 23, 2025).

[12] Carl Richards, "Learning to Deal with the Impostor Syndrome," *The New York Times*, October 26, 2015, https://www.nytimes.com/2015/10/26/your-money/learning-to-deal-with-the-impostor-syndrome.html (last accessed July 23, 2025).

[13] Terry Gross, "Tom Hanks Says Self-Doubt is 'a High Wire Act That We All Walk,'" *Fresh Air* podcast, National Public Radio, April, 26, 2016, https://www.npr.org/2016/04/26/475573489/tom-hanks-says-self-doubt-is-a-high-wire-act-that-we-all-walk (last accessed August 6, 2025).

[14] Vanessa Van Edwards, "Imposter Syndrome: Which of These 9 Types Are You?" Science of People, April 10, 2025, https://www.scienceofpeople.com/impostor-syndrome/ (last accessed July 23, 2025).

Chapter 5

[15] Mallory Stark, "Creating a Positive Professional Image," *Harvard Business School*, June 20, 2005, https://www.library.hbs.edu/working-knowledge/creating-a-positive-professional-image, (last accessed August 6, 2025).

[16] Coleman, *Empowering Yourself*.

[17] Catherine Cote, "Personal Branding: What It is and Why It Matters," *Harvard Business Review*, March, 21, 2024, https://online.hbs.edu/blog/post/personal-branding-at-work (last accessed August 6, 2025).

[18] Stark, "Creating a Positive Professional Image."

[19] Sara Blakely Instagram post, October 16, 2024, https://www.instagram.com/p/DBNISTRx-ak/?img_index=1 , (last accessed August 6, 2025).

[20] Sara Blakely LinkedIn.com profile, https://www.linkedin.com/in/sarablakely27/ (last accessed July 23, 2025).

[21] Roger L. Martin and A.G. Lafley, Playing to Win: How Strategy Really Works (Harvard Business Review Press, 2013).

Chapter 11

[22] Merriam-Webster.com, definition of "strategy," https://www.merriam-webster.com/dictionary/strategy, (last accessed July 23, 2025).

Chapter 12

[23] *Ferris Bueller's Day Off*, directed by John Hughes (Paramount Pictures, 1986).

[24] Theodore Roosevelt quote, Goodreads.com, https://www.goodreads.com/quotes/312751-nothing-in-the-world-is-worth-having-or-worth-doing (last accessed July 23, 2025).

[25] Be Bold, Be Visible, Be the Leader You Were Meant to Be Facebook group: https://www.facebook.com/groups/265115150545457.

www.ingramcontent.com/pod-product-compliance
Lightning Source LLC
Chambersburg PA
CBHW022203090526
44583CB00012BA/287